Manx Electric Railway

Past & Present

GEORGE HOBBS

Loaghtan Books
Caardee
Dreemskerry Hill
Maughold
Isle of Man
IM7 1BE

Published by Loaghtan Books

First published: May 2016

Typesetting and origination by:
Loaghtan Books

Printed and bound by:
Lavenham Press Ltd

Website: www.loaghtanbooks.com

ISBN: 978 1 908060 14 3

Front cover: Paddlebox and trailer 42, plus winter saloon 21 at Bellevue (see page 113 for more information)

Rear cover: Upper: Winter saloon 20 crossing Ramsey Road by the Road Service's Bus depot, Laxey *(Vic Nutton, Courtesy Travel Lens Photographic, 1970s)*; *Lower:* Winter saloon 21 with trailer 41 crossing Ramsey Road *(26 September 2015)*

Title page: Car 16 and trailer unloading at Derby Castle *(Ted Gray, Courtesy Travel Lens Photographic, 1962)*

Introduction, page 3: Open motor 16 and trailer approaching Preston's Crossing *(Vic Nutton, Courtesy Travel Lens Photographic, 1974)*

Introduction, page 4: Upper: Open motor 31 and tunnel car 6 both with trailers at Derby Castle depot *(Courtesy Travel Lens Photographic, 1960s)*; *Lower:* Tunnel car 6 and trailer on siding at Derby Castle with horse cars under the iron shelter *(Vic Nutton, Courtesy Travel Lens Photographic, 1973)*

CONTENTS

Contents

Contents	3
Introduction	3-4
Locations	5-139
Selected Bibliography	140
Acknowledgements	140

INTRODUCTION

The Manx Electric Railway may look as though it is set in a time warp, a seemingly unchanging tramway served by unchanging trams over more than 120 years. This is not the case; the survival of the tramway is due to its continual adaptation over the years. The railway, the island and the people whom the tramway serves have moved with the times. A major change was the takeover of the tramway by the Manx Government in 1957 when the owner, The Manx Electric Railway Company, was practically bankrupt and unable to continue to operate and maintain it.

The environment of the tramway has changed. Like the rest of the world the Isle of Man is not immune to social and economic pressures. Housing developments around the major towns have nibbled at the countryside; villas and bungalows have appeared in rural areas, and tourist facilities, suffering from the onslaught of cheap flights and hotels in warmer climes, have been superseded by residential developments. The farming communities have adapted to more intensive land use. Most significantly the prevalence of private car ownership has led to a decrease in demand and the loss of the year-round tram service, with a concentration on the seasonal leisure market.

The tramway infrastructure has also changed. At Derby Castle the cast iron shelter for the Douglas Corporation horse trams was demolished early in 1980. This was adjacent to the MER terminus and also used by MER passengers. The upper car sheds at Derby Castle (1999) and the shed at Laxey (2009) have been replaced. The tracks were re-laid at Laxey station in 2014 and the Ballure Viaduct, near Ramsey was refurbished in 2015. The power supply has been upgraded with modern solid state replacing the mercury arc rectifiers. Continued expenditure on track replacement and maintenance, including recent installation of concrete sleepers and long welded rail, are now making a visual (and audible) difference compared to the traditional jointed rail on wooden sleeper track.

The infrastructure evolution continues. At the time of writing there are proposals to redevelop Ramsey station (constructed in 1964) to provide an integrated bus-tram interchange, which would remove the inconvenience of the two modes of transport being separated by a few hundred yards. The new proposals, incorporating stainless steel and glass, are not entirely sympathetic to the heritage appearance of the tramway and have generated some adverse reactions from residents and enthusiasts.

Over the years the carriage of goods by tram has also declined. The cessation of the carriage of mail, including the collection of post from the wayside post boxes, took place in 1975 when the Laxey to Ramsey section was closed and the winter service suspended. Fortunately the closure of the northern section of line was not permanent and the line re-opened fully in 1977, although postal collection from the lineside boxes was not resumed. The decline in goods traffic was slow and the author has memories of car exhausts often being carried from Douglas to Ramsey in the conductor's cab on the last tram of the day in the late 1990s.

On board the trams, electronic ticketing came into use in 2015 and it is possible to purchase travel in advance by validating a plastic card which is read by the conductors' portable devices. Data about the tramway's usage can be downloaded and analyzed on the head office computers. This is an integrated system with the Steam Railway and the island's nationalized bus network. It is a far cry from the pre-printed card tickets of the Victorian era.

A major visual change has been the nature of the countryside itself, which is particularly apparent when attempting to replicate an historic view with a modern one. The spread of trees in many areas is astonishing: in some cases open vistas have been replaced by dense woodland with the tramway taking a shady route beneath the trees. In part this may be due to the move away from open fires with the effect that wood is now little valued for home heating.

Sadly, from an enthusiast's point of view the cumulative effect of all these changes over the last few decades has led to a decrease in the number of tramcars required to run services. The past photographs, mainly taken by visiting enthusiasts during their holidays, show a heavy reliance on the open (crossbench) motor cars. At the time of writing only three of the open motors are in the active fleet, although a major restoration project is currently under way to resuscitate car 14. There is unlikely to be a large scale return to open motor usage, unless the Isle of Man experiences a welcome but unexpected return to favour as a holiday destination, or global warming produces balmier climes.

The object of this book is to draw on historic photographs and to demonstrate the changes to the Manx Electric Railway and its environs which have – or have not – occurred over the years. The historic views are not always possible to date accurately, but best estimates have been made.

Taking the same view from the same spot has not always been possible. The increase in foliage and the inclusion of formerly accessible land into private residential property has also restricted the choice of locations. In the past it is clear that photographers took a fairly relaxed attitude to access to railway property, but in the interest of complying with present day attitudes towards health and safety, new photographs have not been taken from the immediate trackside between stops although these could have provided interesting comparisons. On the plus side it is clear that many of the old photographs were taken using a single lens camera whose fixed focal length was very close to the 35mm focal length setting on the author's more modern camera. Accordingly, setting that length and then matching the shot made life simpler.

In some instances exact locations are not readily discernible. For instance, where the upper car shed at Derby Castle was replaced by a new shed the interior bears scant resemblance to the original, so licence has been taken with the precise positioning of the photographs. At Laxey the current car shed is the third one to stand on the site: the first was destroyed by the fire of 1930 and the replacement suffered corrosion, finally being superseded by the present shed in 2009, so identifying exact locations is difficult. Geographically, the text follows the line from Douglas to Ramsey, with locations generally identified by their nearest recognized stop.

Hopefully this trip along the line will be illuminating in terms of illustrating the changes, and comforting in showing the consistency of this fascinating tramway. Long may it continue to serve the island.

One of the pair of 1906 motors (32 or 33) is paired with trailer 61 and awaits departure from Derby Castle. The car set is in the green and white livery of the nationalized organization. In the background stands the cast iron shelter of the Douglas Corporation horse tram terminus, but which carries advertising for the electric railway; behind it is The Strathallan Hotel public house and on the right is the turreted entrance to the pleasure grounds of Derby Castle itself. The fare board on the left shows that a return trip to Snaefell costs a mere eight shillings (40p), considerably less than the 2015 fare of £14.00. *(Vic Nutton, Courtesy Travel Lens Photographic, c1960)*

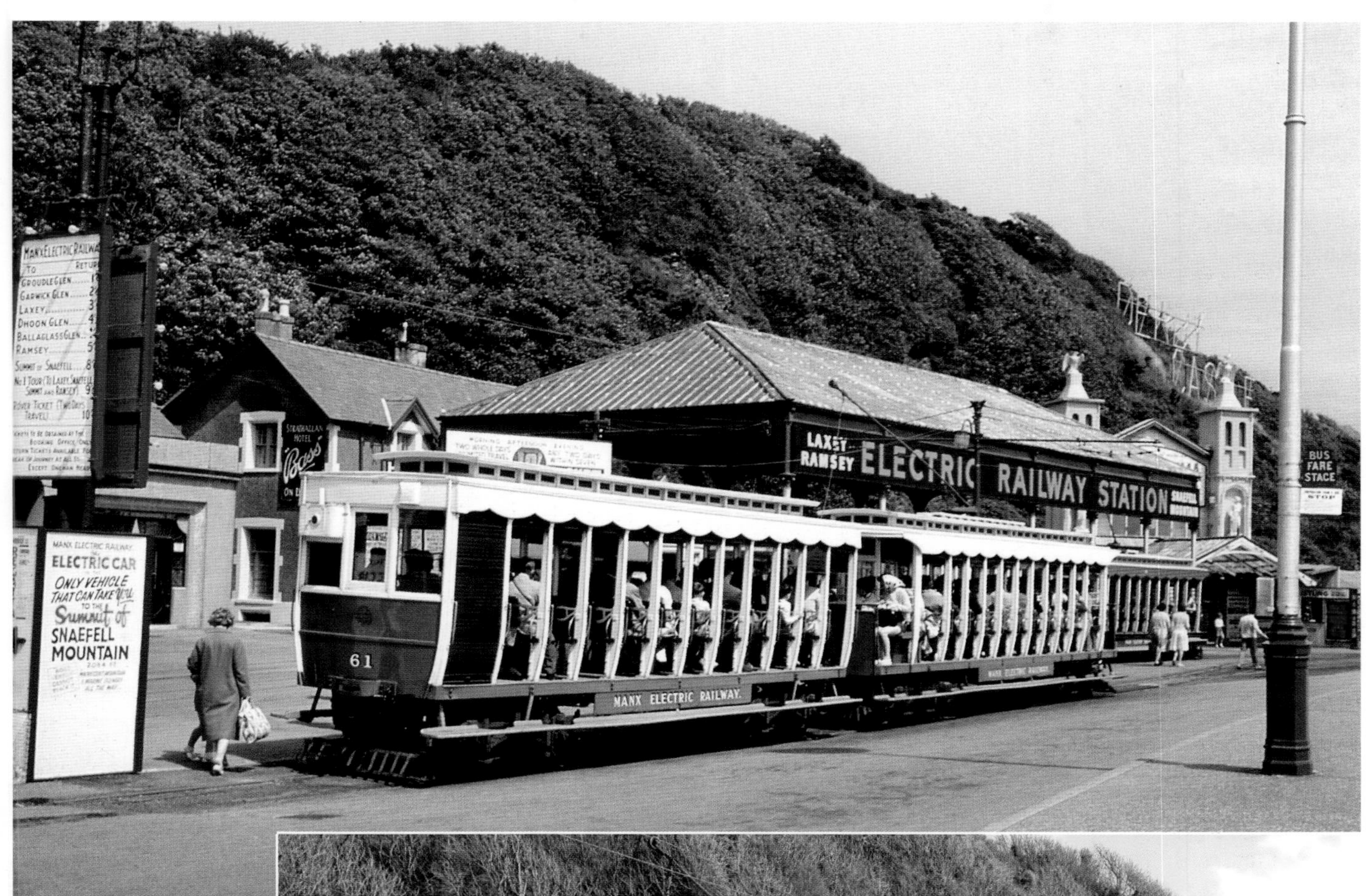

Also seen at the end of the line and waiting to leave is 1893 motor car 2. The change in the background includes the removal of the canopy over the horse tram terminus and the Derby Castle entrance. In the latter location there has been a triple removal as Derby Castle and both versions of Summerland have gone, leaving an unalluring vacant plot. In 1982, the Strathallan Hotel changed its name to the more familiar Terminus Tavern, a very apt title given its situation at the southern end of the Manx Electric Railway. *(25 March 2016)*

Car 28 waits at Derby Castle, probably with an extra service to Laxey, as closed saloons predominated on the scheduled Ramsey services. The car set is completed with a lightweight trailer which, not having full height side stanchions, provides unrestricted views of the countryside. Derby Castle was a busy interchange between the bus services of Douglas Corporation, whose apparently empty double-decker is departing in the background, the Corporation's horse trams and the electric cars of the MER. *(Vic Nutton, Courtesy Travel Lens Photographic, 1964)*

Car 2 waits to depart from Derby Castle. All bus services on the island are now provided by the nationalized Isle of Man Transport organization (Bus Vannin) and, although Derby Castle is no longer a bus terminus, there are adjacent stops on the promenade. The green-painted metal shelter serves both bus and tram passengers and is in stark contrast to the rustic booking office of the MER, which still stands at the terminus, although it has lost its roof decoration. The horse tram terminus makes this a three-way transport interchange. *(25 March 2016)*

One of the two surviving original motor cars from 1893, number 1, is also paired with a lightweight trailer at Derby Castle as it awaits its time to depart. The rapid development of tramway technology in the early days led to the original cars being re-equipped with new bogies after a few years, but the bodywork is original. The original current collection system used bow collectors, as used on the Snaefell line even now, but this was changed to trolley poles over the winter of 1897-8 prior to the Ramsey extension opening. Car 1's clerestory windows have been painted over and the rocker panels lack any fleetname. *(Courtesy Travel Lens Photographic, c1970)*

Car 1 is once again posed at Derby Castle paired with super-lightweight trailer 51, but this time in the siding. Both items of rolling stock are original 1893 specimens. Car 1's clerestory windows have been cleared and its paintwork and lettering are a credit to the tramway. Today is the Manx Heritage Transport Festival and the trams are displayed in the siding as two of the most significant and valued items on the tramway. Accordingly, departure is not imminent and intending passengers are requested to join the next service tram on the adjacent line. *(29 July 2015)*

On the same occasion as the previous historic view (see page 7, top), two car sets are at Derby Castle. In the background car 1 and lightweight trailer are waiting to depart while, nearer the camera, car 29 has completed its run-round manoeuvre and is about to propel the trailer down to form the next service, once number 1 has departed. Behind car 29 is the overall canopy for the Douglas Corporation horse tram service which was demolished in early 1980. *(Courtesy Travel Lens Photographic, c1970)*

At busy times it is still possible for more than one car set to be found at Derby Castle. In this instance there had been a problem with the leading set (car 2 and lightweight trailer 60) as the air brakes had failed and the set had been eased down from the summit at Howstrake on the handbrake with an extra brakeman on the trailer. Flagmen guarded the level crossings on the way down. As the intensive service of the 'Rush Hour on the Railways' special event is operating, the following service comprising open motor 33 and trailer 44 has caught up. The result is a queue of trams waiting to shunt at the terminus. *(5 April 2015)*

Prior to the end of the 1975 season, the Manx Electric Railway held the postal service contract between Douglas and Ramsey. It is almost a quarter past five by the clock on the Strathallan horse tram depot and an Austin van has brought the evening mail bags for the north of the island. The van carries the legend 'Royal Mail' – the Isle of Man Post Office was established as a separate establishment in 1973. Here the mail bags are being loaded into one of the MER vans, which will be attached to the rear of a passenger service to take the bags to the Ramsey sorting office. Sadly this is a scene which is no longer possible to see as the mail now makes the full journey by road. *(Courtesy Travel Lens Photographic, c1970)*

A Vauxhall van attends to the different demands of the tramway. The trolley of car 1 has been giving the conductor a hard time, having depoled several times on its last trip. A van has been dispatched from the depot (visible in the background) with a new brass trolley wheel. Pulling the trolley down and to the side gives easy access for the engineers' department who are using the van roof to reach and effect a replacement with minimal disruption to the service. *(5 April 2015)*

Having arrived at Derby Castle with a southbound service the standard procedure is for the motor car to run round its trailer and shunt it back to the end of the line to load for the return trip. Here one of the 1894 tunnel cars, number 9, is about to couple up to trailer 51 and propel it down to the waiting area. Trailer 51 is one of the original 1893 trailers and is seen in its modified form with end bulkheads. It has subsequently been restored to its original condition, without end bulkheads, and currently carries its historic original livery. In the background Summerland is under construction on the site of the former Derby Castle, dating this picture to around 1970. *(Courtesy Travel Lens Photographic, c1970)*

Summerland was demolished and the site cleared during the tramway's winter closure of 2005-6. After completion of the works the tramway tracks were renewed past the site. This is the end of the first week of the 2015 season and tunnel car 7 is shunting trailer 48 back to the loading area. As is usual at this time of year, new conducting staff are being trained for the coming season and here the instructor is checking that correct procedures are being followed by the trainee who is giving hand signals to the motorman. Female platform staff are rare but not unknown on the MER. *(28 March 2015)*

Winter saloon 20, running without a trailer, passes the entrance to the Derby Castle car shed; the pointwork can be seen on the right. In the distance, a car set waits at Derby Castle to form the next northbound service and there is another recently arrived car set waiting just outside the station to shunt its trailer before drawing down to the loading area. Clearly it is a busy day on the tramway and the absence of a trailer with car 20 is surprising. The tower crane is assisting with the construction work on Summerland so the photographic can be dated to around 1970. *(Courtesy Travel Lens Photographic, c1970)*

Looking from the footpath beside the depot, on the inland side of the line rather than from the promenade side, open motor 32 with trailer 41 is climbing away from Derby Castle and passing over the pointwork leading to the depot. The 'Rush Hour on the Railways' event at Easter is one of the first opportunities in the season to enjoy the open motor cars – if the weather is favourable. Car 32 carries the tramway crest above the headlight; in recent years most repainted cars have not received this embellishment which suits their historic appearance. *(7 April 2015)*

Ratchet car 18 climbs away from Derby Castle past the original Summerland. In view of the complete absence of passengers it is likely that the tram is returning to the depot which is only a few yards away up the hill. On 2 August 1973 Summerland suffered a disastrous fire. Fifty people were killed and eighty injured, so this photograph was taken during the couple of years between opening and destruction, i.e., 1971-3. *(Courtesy Travel Lens Photographic, c.1972)*

Car 1 of 1893 climbs past the site of Summerland with a morning service to Ramsey. Abutting the cliff face in the background, part of the old swimming pool has been retained to assist the stability of the rock face, which might otherwise suffer partial collapse. The second Summerland complex was almost totally demolished during the tramway's winter closure in 2005-6. Slight differences in the gradient allow a reasonably precise location to be determined for this photograph. *(Sara Goodwins, 25 March 2016)*

The lower shed is the original building dating from the opening of the tramway in 1893 and is still in use. At the time of this photograph, the top shed accommodated the principal service trams and the lower shed tended to be used for the less frequently used cars, hence the preponderance of lightweight trailers which are more suited for use in good weather. Four trailers can be distinguished along with an open motor and car 1. A member of the staff sits inside the shed working on a tram component. *(Vic Nutton, Courtesy Travel Lens Photographic, 1964)*

It is a summer Sunday and the museum housed in the leftmost part of the building is operating with its volunteer staff. On these days a display of trams is parked outside the depot and the museum staff are only too pleased to show any visitors around the exhibits which are ideally placed for photography, weather permitting. The lower shed is now normally used for maintenance work and not for day-to-day operations. The tracks have been removed from the part of the building with the windows and the main shed doors are closed. Car 1 stands on the road outside the old paint shop. *(6 September 2015)*

On the left, the bulk of the Summerland complex looms over the tramway. Winter saloon 19 is propelling a trailer uphill. Having finished its duty for the day the car set is being shunted from the terminus at Derby Castle to the car shed and is about to take the facing points into the depot yard. The tower of the Douglas Bay Hotel peeks over the cliff beyond the depot. In the foreground the concrete footbridge which joined Summerland to the seaward side of the promenade frames the tram and the road. This photograph postdates the fire that destroyed the original Summerland, but parts of the structural framework are still visible. *(Vic Nutton, Courtesy Travel Lens Photographic, 1975)*

The present day view is very different. The second incarnation of Summerland has now gone, giving a clear view of the Derby Castle depot. The Douglas Bay Hotel has been displaced by the blue and white building of King Edward Bay House, currently the home of Pokerstars, the on-line gambling business. The wooden original upper sheds of the tram depot have also been replaced by steel portal frame structures. Winter saloon 21 and trailer 40 climb past the depot. Interestingly, the road in front of the photographer is still marked as a 'bus stop' although for many years buses have stopped opposite the tram terminus and not here. *(31 August 2015)*

The top sheds at Derby Castle are the main under-cover storage for the service cars. They were developed in stages, starting in 1894 when the tramway's extension to Laxey required additional car storage facilities. Further shed extensions followed up to 1924, all in a similar wood framed style with light cladding. Gaps in the cladding over the doors allow passage of the trolley wires. Motor car 1, which has climbed up from the lower shed, and open motor 16 pose outside the sheds. The suited gentleman on the front platform of car 1 does not have the appearance of being a regular motorman. *(Courtesy Travel Lens Photographic, 1960s)*

As it is Sunday there is a good display of five trams on the depot fan, in conjunction with the museum opening hours. The 'Electric Railway' illuminated sign on the cliff has been renewed but continues to advertise the tramway's presence, being visible along the whole of the Douglas promenades. At the time of writing (early 2016) the sign is being refurbished once again, this time using latest light emitting diode (LED) technology, showing that the MER is willing to adopt appropriate new technology in the twenty-first century. *(10 May 2015)*

The doors of the top shed stand open and much of the fleet is out working. Inside the shed can be seen car 1 (far left) and several open motors, including 32 and 16 on the right, the closed motor cars generally being used for the principal services. In the siding nearest the sea one of the goods vans is just visible, the bright tyres of its wheels showing that it is currently in use, probably for the postal traffic. *(Courtesy Travel Lens Photographic, 1960s)*

The top sheds at Derby Castle were replaced in 1998 by a new three-bay portal frame steel structure with steel cladding. This is a fairly standard industrial building design adapted to meet the needs of the tramway. The siding which contained the van in the previous photograph has now been removed and, as there is no freight traffic on the MER nowadays, the wagon fleet has been much reduced. As this is a Sunday the MER museum is open and the display outside the new shed includes original motor, car 2, partly obscuring winter saloon 19, 'Royal Trailer' 59 and the tramway's newest motor car, number 33 of 1906. *(24 August 2014)*

For a while in the 1970s car 1 was used for engineers' duties. To provide the motorman with some degree of weather protection, basic windscreens were fitted at either end, which cannot be said to have improved its historic appearance. Behind car 1 is what appears to be an adapted open wagon carrying a substantial tank, presumably filled with weed killer as part of the effort to keep the track clear of vegetation. *(Courtesy Travel Lens Photographic, 1970s)*

Standing on the adjacent track is the other surviving original motor car from 1893, car 2. Looking resplendent with white walled tyres this tram is certainly in good condition for a vehicle in its thirteenth decade of operation. Note the wooden chock under the nearest wheel: the handbrake is on but the slope down to the shed is steep and the tram is heavy. In the background the remains of the Summerland complex have been a local eyesore since 2005. *(29 July 2015)*

31
29
16
ELECTRIC RAILWAY
44

Inside the old shed at Derby Castle paddlebox motor 26's front bogie is receiving attention. As he is wearing the brown dust jacket of the platform staff, this is probably the driver checking the axlebox oil level prior to taking the tram out on service. The old shed, with its wooden columns, is very open and a good illustration of the North American terminology, 'car barn', which is applied to tram sheds. Interestingly, the location of the fleet number varies from above to below the headlights on cars 31 and 29, with the latter displaying the tramway crest on the dash panel as well as the number. *(Courtesy Travel Lens Photographic, 1960s)*

The modern steel-framed shed is not quite as open as the original, with corrugated steel walls allowing pedestrian access sideways but restricting the free flow of air above head height. In the middle bay of the shed, open motor 16, wearing green and white livery, is parked next to trailer 44. Car 16 first acquired the 'historic' green livery in 1998, never having been repainted in this colour during the period when it was being applied across the fleet in the early days of the nationalized tramway. It has now operated in green for nearly twenty years. Its companion trailer, 60, first acquired its green livery in 2000. *(6 September 2015)*

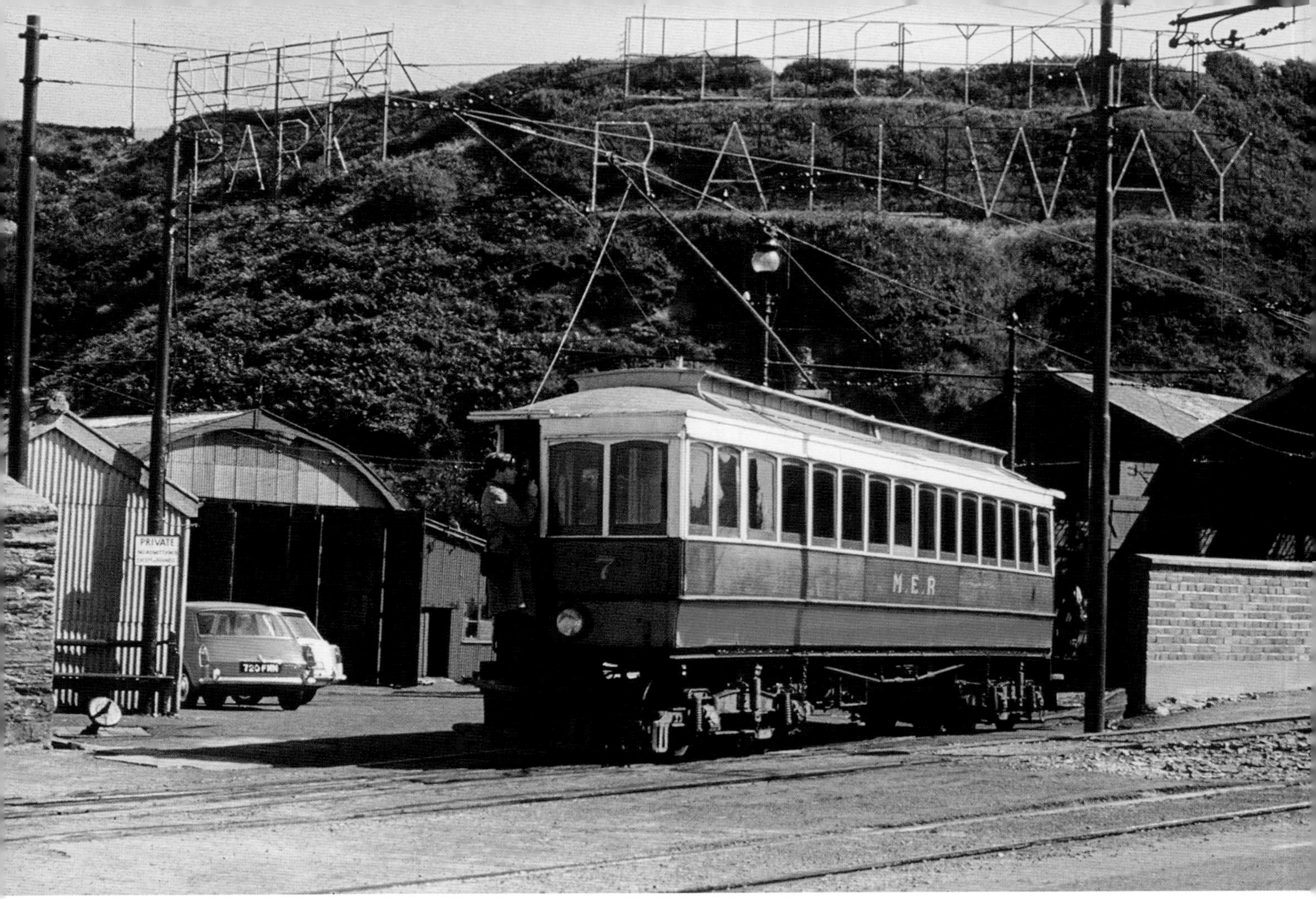

Tunnel car 7 is shunting into Derby Castle depot at the end of a turn of duty. The conductor, complete with cash bag, stands on the back step of the tram and holds the trolley rope ready to help guide the trolley wheel through the next frog in the overhead wire. Car 7 carries a simplified livery, with no embellishments in the form of lining out, and the most basic form of the fleetname possible. This economic style was common in the last days of the MER before nationalization in 1957, so maybe car 7 has not been repainted since then? *(Courtesy Travel Lens Photographic, 1960s)*

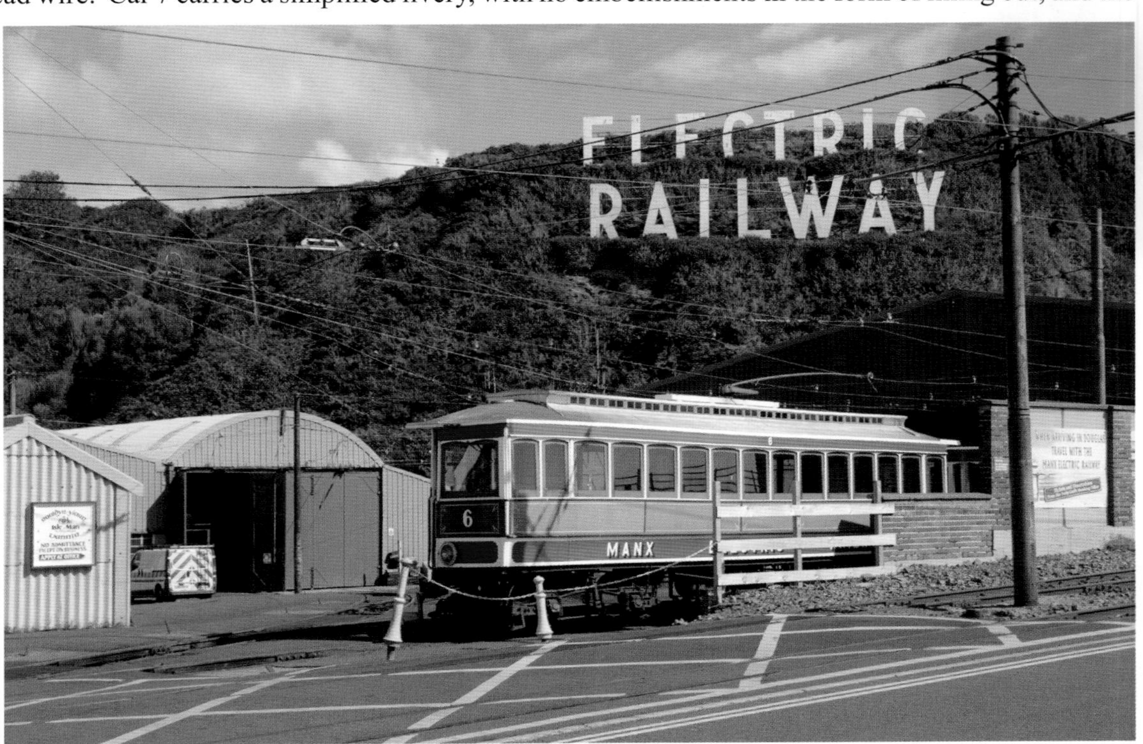

Standing in the same location is sister tunnel car 6. The tunnel cars were built with two piece windscreens, with a central vertical divider. In the 1960s, to improve the motorman's visibility, the windscreens were replaced with large single panes. To improve the ride, these cars also received additional suspension in the form of the sprung struts fitted to the mid-side of the bogies. Just visible behind is the green and white paintwork of a trailer, which must be number 60 as it is the only trailer currently carrying these colours. On the cliffs behind the depot the illuminated sign for 'Onchan Park' has now been removed, although the 'Electric Railway' sign still proudly proclaims the local attraction. *(31 August 2015)*

Inside Derby Castle top shed a pair of open motors is parked. The Manx Electric cars do not usually carry advertising (unlike the Douglas Corporation horse cars) but number 15 proudly proclaims on the dash 'Special this year. No increase in fares'. The negative implication being that increased fares are to be expected! There are also advertising panels on the footboard. Perhaps number 15 spends much of its time parked in the siding by the Derby Castle booking office as a mobile advertising hoarding? *(Courtesy Travel Lens Photographic, 1960s)*

With the replacement of the Derby Castle top sheds with new steel portal-frame structures in 1998 it is difficult to find any reference points to match the previous location exactly. In the new shed tunnel car 9, fitted with special illuminations, is parked with a trailer. Car 9 was first fitted with illuminations in 1993 to coincide with the MER centenary celebrations; the current style was adopted in 2004. On the wall (top left) is an array of light bulbs which give an instant indication to staff as to whether the wires are live or not. *(10 May 2015)*

Car 9 and trailer head north past the burnt-out remains of the first Summerland, destroyed in 1973. This photograph dates from shortly after the fire and, as such, has rarity value, justifying its use despite its relatively poor quality. The desolate remains are a sad backdrop to the tramway which passes on the seaward side. At the time of the fire Summerland had been open for just over two years and its destruction was the worst fire in the British Isles since the end of the Second World War. *(George Hearse, Courtesy Travel Lens Photographic, August 1973)*

Ascending the line, winter saloon 19 is coupled with wheelchair accessible trailer 56, which appears on ordinary services by prior arrangement with the traffic staff. This trailer was rebuilt in 1995 on the underframe of a typical open trailer, and may also be reserved for private hire. This view is a bit nearer to the terminus than the previous one. The demolition, not just of the remains of Summerland but also its successor which operated from 1978 to 2004, has left a site which is neither beautiful nor useful at the northern end of the Douglas promenades. *(31 August 2015)*

Beyond Derby Castle car sheds the tramway climbs up past Port Jack, crossing the culverted stream from Port Jack Glen which enters the cove via a waterfall. The sharp curve and steep incline across the road junction can require careful handling, especially with wet, greasy rails. Looking down from the terrace outside the Douglas Bay Hotel, a tunnel car and trailer are climbing past the parade of shops and are about to cross the road junction. On the road, a tour coach heads down towards Douglas, passing a police emergency call post on the edge of the footpath. *(Vic Nutton, Courtesy Travel Lens Photographic, 1964)*

Winter saloon 22 and trailer 40 pass the Port Jack parade. The Douglas Bay Hotel was demolished in 1988 and the present-day photograph is taken from the top of the steps leading to King Edward Bay House, an office block built on the site of the hotel. The dormer windows have grown larger but the parade of shops is still recognisably the same. The age of the universal mobile phone has rendered the police call post superfluous and mobile phone masts have replaced call boxes as street furniture. *(6 September 2015)*

Also captured from the vantage point of the Douglas Bay Hotel, winter saloon 21 and its trailer cross the road and swing round the head of the Port Jack inlet. There is a fish and chip shop on the corner, but it seems to be rather anonymous at this time: advertisements for well known soft drinks are evidently more important than the name of the establishment. *(Courtesy Travel Lens Photographic, c1970)*

The Douglas Bay Hotel has long gone, replaced by King Edward Bay House, lying at the start of the King Edward Road. This is the home of on-line gambling business Pokerstars. Originally called Skandia House it was previously the offices of Skandia Insurance. Winter saloon 19 and trailer 47 take the curve on a late summer's day. The road junction has been improved to accommodate the increased traffic levels and pedestrian refuges added at mid-width. Three generations of the Handley family have provided the traditional meal from the Port Jack Chippy and the name is now prominently displayed. During the winter season 2015-6 the track was re-laid across this junction, with considerable disruption to road traffic between the Promenades and Onchan. *(31 August 2015)*

Winter saloon 20 and trailer 43 are passing Port Jack with a well-laden service. The climb here, at 1 in 24, is one of the steepest on the MER and, combined with the sharp curvature across the road junction, trams will only stop at Port Jack in the downhill direction. Unusually for the MER the parade of shops runs parallel to the tramway which makes it the nearest that the tramway comes to street running over its whole length. *(Courtesy Travel Lens Photographic, c1970)*

Winter saloon 22 and trailer 41 are climbing past the shops at Port Jack with a northbound service. Although the location is similar, the positions of traction poles have changed and there is no longer an uninterrupted view of the tram. Shoppers and passengers are now requested to 'Please use walk ways' rather than the tramway ballast. The Half Moon Cafe has now been supplanted by a more exotic Tapas Restaurant and the presence of a beauty parlour instead of the Silver Dollar Amusement arcade behind the trailer is also a sign of the times. *(31 August 2015)*

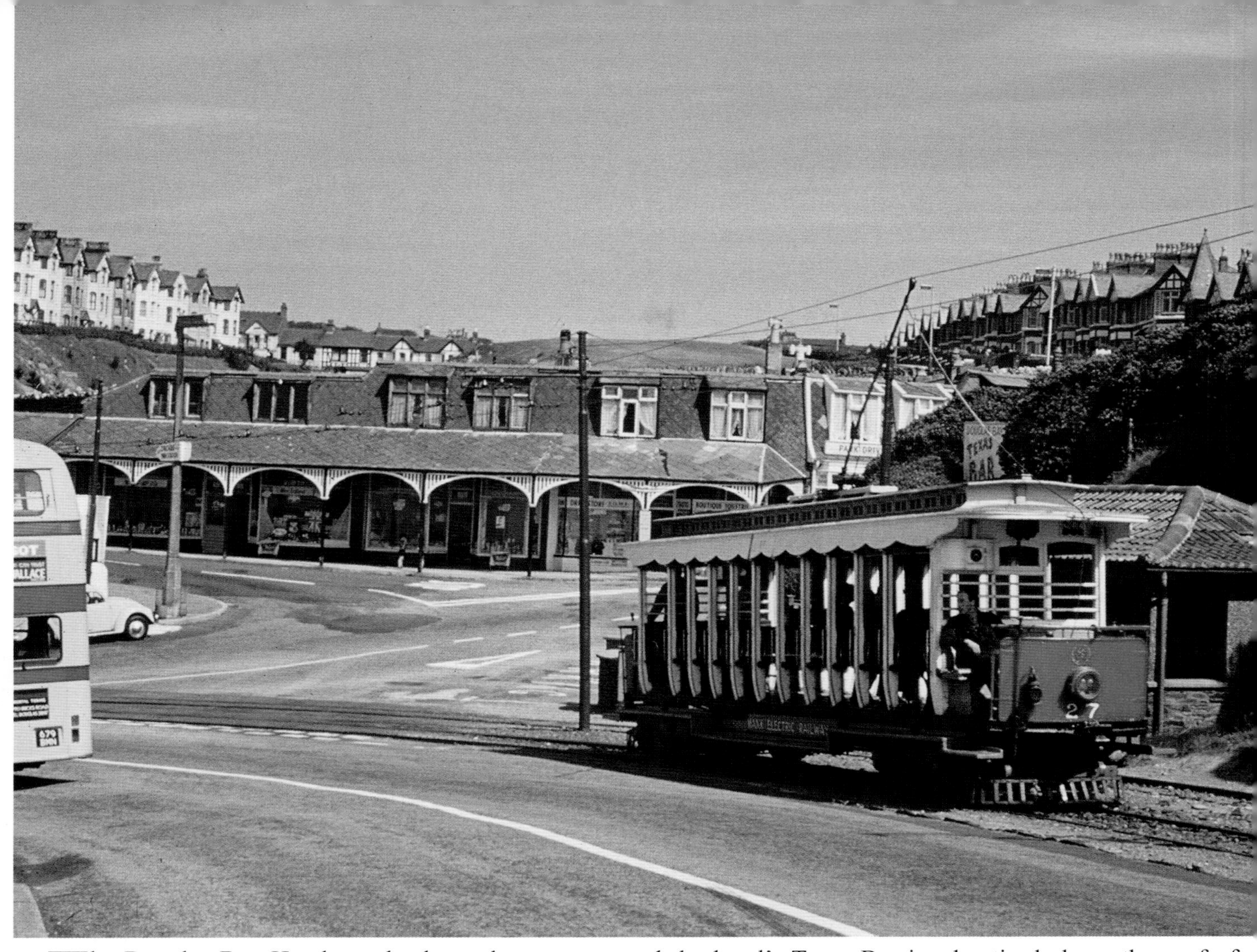

The Douglas Bay Hotel stands above the tramway and the hotel's Texas Bar is advertised above the roof of open motor car 27 as it coasts downhill to Derby Castle. Car 27 carries an oil lamp on the rear dash, which would maintain a warning of the tram's position should the power fail after dark. Meanwhile, on the road a Douglas Corporation bus, also heading downhill, has just passed the photographer. 679 BMN was one of a pair of AEC Regent Vs with forward entrance Willowbrook bodywork which joined the fleet in 1965, indicating that the photograph was probably taken in the late 1960s or early 1970s. *(Courtesy Travel Lens Photographic, c1970)*

Winter saloon 20 and trailer 46 are heading past the same spot. The public convenience still stands behind the trams, but the junction has now acquired the expected yellow box junction markings as well as bollards. Box junctions were introduced in the UK in 1967, and presumably the Isle of Man followed with similar legislation. The impressive buildings on the skyline behind the tram flank Port Jack Glen, a pleasant public park which the average tram passenger can easily be unaware of. *(31 August 2015)*

This photograph can be dated by the mix of currencies in use. Candy floss is available for 5p (one shilling), whereas the children's ride is available for only 6d, which would have been half the price of the candy floss in old money. As decimal currency was introduced in February 1971 then the photograph was probably taken shortly after the new money became available. Climbing away from Derby Castle is winter saloon 22 with trailer. Note that the conductor is on the trailer footboard collecting fares – a procedure that is now forbidden on health and safety grounds. *(Tony Wilson, Courtesy Travel Lens Photographic, 1971)*

Winter saloon 20 and trailer 46 climb past the parade of shops at Port Jack with a northbound service. Additional traction poles have been provided here and the nearest one supports a Manx Electric Railway stop flag. New flags featuring a blue and white design were introduced in 2015 replacing the severely faded red flags installed more than a decade previously. Additional safety features are the tarmac foot crossings and signage. Compared with the previous view there has been a huge increase in the volume of private car use. *(31 August 2015)*

Car 7 and trailer descend past the white-painted boundary wall of the Douglas Bay Hotel. Behind the tram, the skeleton for the advertising lights for the White City amusement park stands on the headland. In its heyday, traffic to and from White City justified running short-working trams from Derby Castle to Onchan Head. Demand was so great that a manned ticket office was provided, as collecting all the fares on such a short run was difficult. *(Vic Nutton, Courtesy of Travel Lens Photographic, 1964)*

Winter saloon 19 and trailer 47 descend towards Port Jack. The Douglas Bay Hotel was demolished in 1988 and the site stood empty for many years before being replaced by an office block, now known as King Edward Bay House. It is the home of the electronic gambling company, Pokerstars: an example of the Isle of Man's diversity of business in the 21st Century. The White City amusement park closed in 1985 and has now been replaced by a housing development. The advertisement lights are long gone. *(31 August 2015)*

One of the paddlebox open motors heads north past Onchan Head with open trailer 55. In the background is the café/restaurant most recently known as *The Heights*, although there have been many name changes over the years. The crossover is the first one north of Derby Castle, only a few minutes away, and, somewhat surprisingly, it is still in situ. *(Tony Wilson, Courtesy of Travel Lens Photographic, 1960s)*

Winter Saloon 20 and trailer 46 head north at the same location. The house on the left in the old photograph still exists but is hidden behind the development of new bungalows. The tramway crossover is in the same position. There is no tramway traffic to White City, the site of which is behind the hedge on the right, but there are far more cars. *(August 31 2015)*

Open motor 33 and trailer are heading north past the Harbour Road crossing. In the background the extent of the White City amusement park is evident with the wooden rollercoaster prominently located near the road junction. The White City illuminated sign framework is silhouetted against the sea and the tower of the Douglas Bay Hotel can be seen on the extreme right. Once again the undeveloped sites near the Onchan Head tram stop on the opposite side of King Edward Road to The White City are visible. *(Vic Nutton, Courtesy Travel Lens Photographic, 1964)*

Standing where the photographer of the old picture stood was not possible as it is now in the garden of a private residence. Tunnel car 7, with matching trailer 48, is heading north. The site of the White City amusement park now has houses on it and the roofs of the properties behind the tram give no indication of the site's commercial usage. The view over Douglas Bay has improved though. *(31 August 2015)*

Heading down the hill towards Derby Castle is ratchet car 18 with trailer. On the left is *Churchill's Café* which gave its name to the stop, although by the date of the photograph it was known as *The Sizzler, Café Royale*. On the right is the Majestic Hotel, opened in 1922, with its extensive grounds. The hotel's owner, Mr Basil Jackson, lived at Far End House, which gave its name to another MER stop a bit further up the hill. King Edward Road stretches into the distance and the King Edward Bay golf course occupies the hill behind the houses built alongside the road. *(Vic Nutton, Courtesy of Travel Lens Photographic, 1967)*

Again the previous view was taken from a location which is now the private garden of a house, so the present-day view is taken from a lower level, nearer the junction of Harbour Road with King Edward Road. Tunnel car 7 and matching blue and white trailer 48 are also nearing journey's end. At the time of the photograph the café was a restaurant called *The Heights*, but it has carried a variety of names down the years, including *Café Royal(e)*, *Julian's*, *Boncomptes* and *The Water Margin*. The site of the Majestic Hotel is now occupied by the luxurious Majestic Apartments. *(31 August 2015)*

The building in the left foreground is Far End House which was the residence of the owner of the Majestic Hotel; the hotel's tower is on the left of King Edward Road above the eaves of Far End House. There are still green fields separating Onchan from Douglas and the road is devoid of motor traffic. An unidentified winter saloon leads trailer 44 downhill towards Derby Castle. On the opposite side of the street from the hotel *Churchill's Café* (or, depending on the exact date, one of its successors) stands above the road. *(Courtesy Travel Lens Photographic, 1960s)*

Winter saloon 20 and trailer 46 coast down the line towards Derby Castle on a bright summer's day. The Braeside stop now sports a modern steel shelter, which serves both bus and tram passengers, the street lighting arrangements have altered and road traffic levels have increased. The hedge between the tramway and the service road on the right is higher, but it is apparent that home extensions have occurred to many of the properties. The tower of the Majestic Hotel was swept away during the redevelopment leading to the modern Majestic Apartments. At the time of the photograph the café continued to offer sustenance from its position above the road. *(31 August 2015)*

Running single motor, tunnel car 5 has just arrived at the Howstrake Holiday Camp stop. On the right the concrete shelter advertises the camp and stop name, providing protection from the weather at this somewhat exposed spot on the top of the headland. Intending passengers need to brave the traffic to cross the road and board their tram, however traffic was both slower and more sparse fifty years ago. *(Tony Wilson, Courtesy of Travel Lens Photographic, 1960s)*

At the same location the same tram is now in charge of a trailer. However, the holiday camp has long been closed and the shelter is now in such a state of dilapidation that it has been necessary to fence it off for health and safety reasons. It is interesting to note the differences in the livery of the tram. The number now appears on the end upper panel, rather than the lower. There are detail changes in the lining out of the panels, including a change from yellow to white and the step edges are now highlighted in yellow. The tramway is not frozen in time. *(15 August 2015)*

Climbing to the summit of the line on its way from Groudle, tunnel car 6 rounds the curve at Howstrake. Behind the tram is the impressive entrance gatehouse to the Howstrake Holiday Camp which used to lie below the headland overlooking Groudle Beach to the north. On its lower nearside car 6 retains the bracket to carry an oil lamp from the days when this feature was essential after dark. *(Courtesy Travel Lens Photographic, 1960s)*

Sister tunnel car 7, substantially rebuilt in 2009-10 and carrying blue and white livery, is also bound for Douglas. Nothing remains of the holiday camp gatehouse above ground level, but from the footway it is possible to see the foundations in the undergrowth beyond the fence. Little remains of the camp buildings. The traction pole supporting the pull-off wires on the curve is still in use, although now reinforced with a guy wire. *(Sara Goodwins, 15 August 2015)*

Car 1 is one of the original trio of power cars used at the start of services on the Manx Electric Railway on 7 September 1893. Here she is seen coasting downhill towards the original terminus at Groudle Glen having just passed the stop at Groudle Old Road. King Edward Road, which runs parallel to the tramway, was opened as a toll road at the same time as the tramway. Originally named Marine Drive, the road name was changed at the time of the visit of King Edward VII and Queen Alexandra in 1902 when they travelled to Ramsey by tram (using what is now called the Royal Trailer, No 59). *(Vic Nutton, courtesy of Travel Lens Photographic, 1964)*

The encroachment of undergrowth has made it difficult to replicate the view. Taken from halfway up an overgrown bank tunnel car 5 and trailer 41 have just passed the Groudle Old Road stop *en route* to Groudle Glen. For once the vegetation provides an interesting vignette, with the brightly lit tramcar nicely framed. Prior to its repaint, car 5 carried the company title in Manx Gaelic, *Raad-Yiarn Lectragh Vannin*. It is the only car to have received this treatment. *(15 August 2015)*

Car 30 has crossed over from the northbound to the southbound line, the pole has been swung and the conductor is leaning on the Douglas end of trailer 36 to push it past the crossover. After this, car 30 will cross back to the northbound line and the conductor will re-attach the trailer to the motor ready for the return trip. There is no kerb between the road and the tramway and prospective passengers are happily waiting on the road by the sign which reads 'Road Vehicles'. Not a recommended course of action in today's traffic conditions. *(Vic Nutton, Courtesy Travel Lens Photographic, 1960s)*

Tunnel car 7 and trailer 48 are heading north and are about to stop at Groudle Glen. Shunting of trams still takes place here, but not quite as often as in the past. In the peak summer season the Groudle Glen Steam Railway operates a Wednesday evening service and some trams are turned here. The railway is a pleasant stroll away down the glen and the combination of the MER and the steam train make an enjoyable evening's outing from Douglas. On the grass bank beyond the waiting shelter, the station name is spelt out in large white concrete letters, a feature dating from the line's centenary in 1993. The window visible in the shelter belongs to the ticket office, long disused but formerly staffed at this once busy location. *(2 August 2015)*

Paddlebox motor 27 and trailer depart from Groudle Glen for Douglas on a sunny day. The conductor swings along the side of the tram on his fare collection duty, requiring some athletic manoeuvring over the stepped footboards. On the traction pole to the left the road sign for a narrow bridge appears – no worry for the trams with their own track but the viaduct is of restricted width. The Groudle Hotel stands on the right and the parked cars may have brought patrons. After a sporadic final season the Groudle Glen Railway closed in 1962, re-opening in 1986 after rebuilding by volunteers. *(Ted Gray, Courtesy of Travel Lens Photographic, August 1962)*

A busy scene at Groudle Glen. On the left, open motor 26 is having its trolley turned. Probably this car has just shunted the trailer which is being coupled up ready to return to Douglas. On the nearer track, car 2 waits its time. Note the ladder suspended along the nearside of this tram; this and the rather dilapidated state of the paintwork indicate that it may be in use by the engineers. By the toll house in the background, a southbound winter saloon has paused and its driver has descended from his cab to wait until the line is clear. *(George Hearse, Courtesy Travel Lens Photographic, 1970s)*

The 2016 Rush Hour on the Railways event started on Good Friday with a parallel run by winter saloon 20 and open motor 16 from Derby Castle to Groudle Glen. Looking from the Ramsey end the car numbers made an appropriate '2016'. After reversing at Groudle, but not swapping tracks, the two trams set off back to Douglas. From the Douglas end the sequence '1620' has no relevance, but the synchronized operation is a rare occurrence. To avoid interference with scheduled services an early start was needed and the pair had to return to Derby Castle before the 09:40 departure of the first Ramsey car. With number 16 being the lowest double-digit numbered car in service, the previous matching year would have been 1933: 2019 is not so far away though! The hotel on the right latterly traded as a restaurant, *La Casa*, but the building is now for sale following its closure. *(25 March 2016)*

GROUDLE VIADUCT

Car 19 heading towards Ramsey with trailer and box van 12 is just leaving the sharp curve over the Groudle Glen viaduct and is about to start the climb up to Halfway. At this time the Manx Electric Railway carried the mail, and the addition of a van behind the passenger trailer provided accommodation for the mail bags. Shunting the van as well as the trailer to reverse the order of the vehicles added an extra effort at the termini. Unusually, car 19 carries 'MER' on its upper side panels as well as 'Manx Electric Railway' on the rocker panels. *(Ted Gray, Courtesy Travel Lens Photographic, August 1962)*

Rebuilt tunnel car 7 and trailer 48 in matching blue and white livery have crossed the Groudle Glen viaduct. The viaduct soars well above the floor level of the glen and its true height is not obvious to anyone travelling by tram or car. Unusually for the MER, the overhead is supported from side arm brackets. The mail now travels by road van, having left the MER with the cessation of the winter service in 1975. Occasionally a mail van is appended for special events, usually carrying specially franked postal covers which appeal to the philatelists. *(27 July 2015)*

From the north side of the viaduct the tramway commences a long climb up Lhen Coan, with the road running parallel all the way to Halfway. Coasting down the slope with a Douglas-bound service are 'paddlebox' open motor 25 and an unidentified trailer. The motorman will be applying the brakes to slow the car set for the sharp curve over the Groudle Glen viaduct. *(Ted Gray, Courtesy Travel Lens Photographic, August 1962)*

Tunnel car 6 and trailer 44 are making the same measured descent down Lhen Coan and will shortly enter the sharp curve and cross the viaduct. It is early afternoon in the height of summer, but the increased height of the trees now puts the trams in shadow. Pole 123, immediately behind the tram, has unequal length bracket arms, this feature giving fixed-head trolleys smoother passage round sharp curves and reducing the potential for depoling. *(15 August 2015)*

Only one halt exists on the long climb up Lhen Coan from Groudle Glen to Halfway and that is about mid-way at Eskadale where Bibaloe Beg Road climbs away inland from the tramway. When built in 1894, the tramway and the road were both driven through what had been open country and there were few nearby houses or farms to serve; indeed the stretch between Eskadale and Halfway is the greatest between any two stops along the line. Winter saloon 19 and trailer are seen ascending from Groudle Glen a few poles south of Eskadale. *(Vic Nutton, Courtesy Travel Lens Photographic, 1964)*

The 1964 picture appears to have been taken from a rocky outcrop above the MER on the inland side of the line. Not an easy location to reach with the increased tree growth. Accordingly, the present-day picture is taken from ground level on the opposite side of the road. Winter saloon 20 and trailer 47 have just taken the bend and are set to tackle the next part of the climb. The route of the tramway round Groudle Glen follows a large hairpin bend: the Groudle Glen Railway station is just as easily accessed by a short walk along a footpath from here as by taking the path from the Groudle Glen stop itself. *(15 August 2015)*

After the climb up from Groudle via Eskadale, the tramway reaches Baldromma (also known as The Liverpool Arms, after the nearby pub on the main road, or Halfway – a reference to its location between Derby Castle and Laxey). Here the tracks cross the main A2 Douglas to Ramsey road at a light-controlled level crossing, performing an S-bend across the road. A northbound service is headed by winter saloon 19 with trailer and post van in tow: the traffic light post is just visible on the left of the picture. As noted on page 38, car 19 carries fleetnames on both side panels. *(Courtesy Travel Lens Photographic, 1960s)*

Travelling in the same direction, paddlebox open motor No 26 and trailer are on the crossing. Interestingly above the traction and feeder current wires there is an extra wire on each side which terminate on either side of the crossing. On the right is a telegraph pole: the telephone wires pass above the MER overhead. The additional pairs of wires prevent a broken or loose telephone wire from coming into contact with the much higher voltage line of the MER. Were they to do so the current would severely damage the local telephone system. *(Courtesy Travel Lens Photographic, 1960s)*

The present-day scene is clearly recognisable, even though the old-fashioned traffic signs are long gone and the now familiar modern variety stand in their place. Tunnel car 6 and trailer 44 make their way towards Ramsey with a northbound service. The houses in the background, near the Baldromma stop, are little changed. The telegraph pole has gone as the wires are probably buried underground, so there is no need for the guard wires above the MER overhead. *(15 August 2015)*

About half a mile along the main A2 road from Baldromma, the tramway stop at Baldrine boasts a shelter, whose windows appear to be boarded up, and a post box. Car 2 and trailer are leaving with a southbound service, with the motorman dressed in the traditional brown dust jacket. On the opposite side of the line, a red-coated lady and her companion wait for the next northbound tram; with the more intensive tram service operated at that time their expedition will soon be under way. *(Vic Nutton, Courtesy Travel Lens Photographic, 1964)*

Once again the previous location was not practical for the present-day photograph, so this picture has been taken from the church car park on the opposite side of the line. Tunnel car 5 and trailer 41 are passing the Baldrine stop – the outline of the waiting hut can just be distinguished behind the tree on the right – and the motorman is applying power for the next part of the run towards Douglas. Traction pole 215 is one of the distinctive and durable cast iron poles originally supplied to the Douglas Southern Electric Tramway which ran along the Marine Drive between Douglas Head and Port Soderick between 1896 and 1939. Many of the poles were acquired by the MER after the Second World War, and continue in use today. *(15 August 2015)*

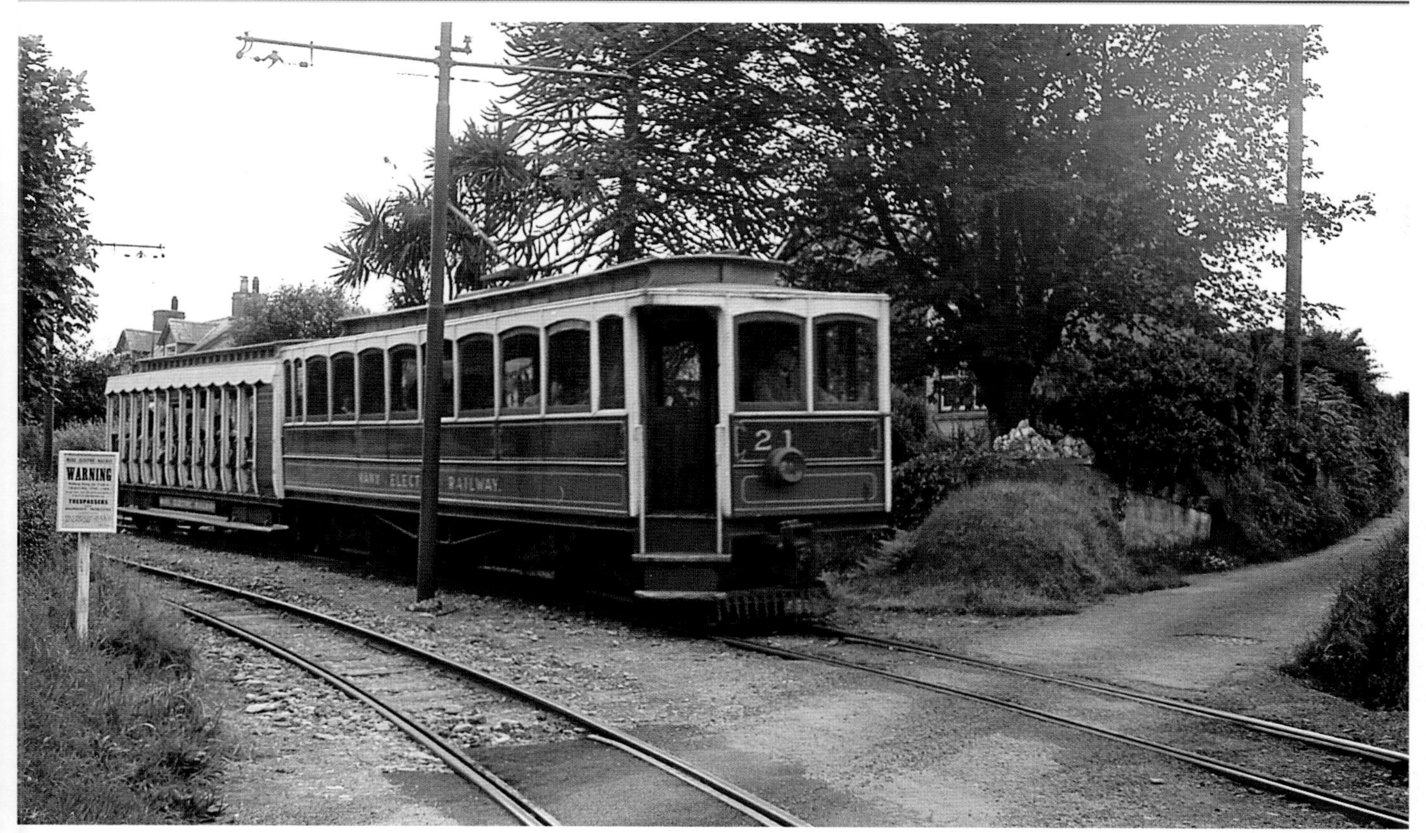

Immediately after Baldrine, the Manx Electric Railway swings inland to pass nearer the head of Garwick Glen, whilst the A2 road dips down into the glen itself. A few poles beyond Baldrine the line crosses the Old Packhorse Road (Upper). This was the location of the now discontinued stop of Sunnycott, which was named after a nearby house. On the left a prominent notice issues a warning against trespassing on the MER. As similar notices do not appear in photographs at other locations, it begs the question of whether there was a particular problem here. *(Vic Nutton, Courtesy Travel Lens Photographic, 1967)*

Sister car 22 and trailer 40 are on their way to Ramsey. Mirrors have been positioned on the corners here to aid visibility for both motormen and road users, and the red and white striped edging of one can just be seen through the windows of the tram. The hedges and trees have grown, the house behind the trailer is now obscured and the trees bordering the lane create the false impression that there is a bridge over the highway. Although trespassing is not encouraged on the MER there is no notice here now. *(Sara Goodwins, 15 August 2015)*

A short distance south of Sunnycott this photograph is taken from the front bench of an open motor car. The driver of southbound tunnel car 7 gives a friendly wave to his colleague who is on the photographer's left. Car 7's trailer is almost obscured by the tram, but its footboard is just visible to the left of the traction pole. The open motor on which the photographer is riding will shortly pass Sunnycott and begin the descent into the upper part of Garwick Glen. *(Courtesy Travel Lens Photographic, 1960s)*

The photographer was not able to arrange for a similar conjunction of trams so the present-day photograph is taken from the vicinity of the level crossing itself. Tunnel car 5 and trailer 41 are approaching with a service for Douglas. The trailer's presence is again confirmed by the footboard visible by the traction pole. Although the motorman is not waving this is not a sign of unfriendliness; he is keeping a watchful eye open for traffic on the crossing – and undoubtedly the antics of the photographer as well. *(Sara Goodwins, 15 August 2015)*

For many years Garwick Glen was owned by the Manx Electric Railway, and tourist entertainments were provided here, including sports and refreshments. To cater for this trade the impressive station facilities seen here were provided. The kiosk, with its lowered counter, advertises cigarettes around its eaves, but may offer confectionery as well. There is a large weighing machine in the station which, although a typical fitment on railway stations at that time, seems a little odd for a station catering almost exclusively for tourists and day trippers. The crossover behind the photographer allowed cars bringing pleasure seekers to terminate here and return to Douglas. The station seems strangely deserted on what is clearly a fine day. Perhaps car 32 is the first tram of the day? *(Courtesy Travel Lens Photographic, 1950s)*

The present-day comparison shows how little remains of the formerly well-kept station. In the left foreground the point blades are in the same location as in the previous picture, although better weed control improves their visibility. The position of the station buildings can be determined from the break in the bank at the side of the line, but the return to nature is almost complete. Out of sight under the trees there is a small wall, and an overgrown path still leads down to the main coast road in the glen. No tram is shown in this picture as it would be a tight squeeze for the photographer between the tram and the bank. *(26 September 2015)*

Tunnel car 5 is seen leaving Garwick Glen station and entering the curve with a Douglas-bound service. Behind the tram the notice advertises Garwick Glen and Caves. Tourists were informed of the existence of 'smugglers caves' adjacent to the small beach at the seaward end of the glen. The sharp curves at the head of the glen cause tram wheels to squeal, which can alert passengers waiting at the adjacent stops of Baldrine or Ballagawne of the impending arrival of their next tram. *(Vic Nutton, Courtesy Travel Lens Photographic, 1967)*

Once again the location of the previous view cannot easily be replicated, without trespassing on the line. Open motor car 33, unusually running with closed trailer, number 58, is leaving Garwick with a service for Douglas. It is TT week, so a special high-intensity service of trams, using all available rolling stock, is operating to the delight of motorcycle and tramway enthusiasts. At this time of year the tramway comes into its own, providing mass transport to and from spectator points on the course. *(7 June 2015)*

Standing by the bus stop on the far side of the road the photographer has captured open motor 29 and lightweight trailer heading towards Douglas. The road sign is one placed by the RAC, dating from an era where the universal provision of road signs by local authorities had not yet come into being. Traffic on the main coast road is conspicuous by its absence. In the distance is the tower of Lonan new church (All Saints), stranded, as one local said, 'like Noah's Ark on its hill'. *(Courtesy Travel Lens Photographic, 1960s)*

Winter saloon 20 and trailer 47 are about to cross Ballagawne Road; traffic on the main road is noticeably heavier – annoyingly so for a photographer trying for a shot like this. The road sign, now provided by the highways department, still points to Creg ny Baa, but remains interesting as it states that this road is the C26. Given the minor road nature of many Manx A roads the significance of this classification is strange: in UK usage 'C' roads are 'County Roads', but numbers are rarely displayed. There are no counties on the island, so why is this one so honoured? The tram stop sign is affixed to the outside of the shelter and not to the traction pole. *(17 October 2015)*

After leaving Garwick Glen the tramway rejoins the main A2 road at Ballagawne, running parallel with the coast road for the next half mile or so. Northbound the sharp curve and restricted sight lines for the level crossing with Ballagawne Road require a slow approach to the stop. The minor road, behind the photographer, is signposted for Creg ny Baa, which lies on the TT circuit and the mountain road. Open motor 32 and trailer are heading south and about to cross Ballagawne Road. *(Vic Nutton, Courtesy Travel Lens Photographic, 1964)*

Winter saloon 21 and trailer 41 at virtually the same spot. The grass bank between the tramway and the main road has been trimmed and the houses have received attention, looking very smart under their new paint. The permanent way is in good fettle complementing the area's neat appearance. In the distance, to the right of the tramway, a major housing development has sprung up at Ballastowell on the southern margins of the Laxey area. Nearer to hand an extra house has been inserted between the two dwellings on the main road. *(26 September 2015)*

At Ballabeg the tramway once again crosses the A2 coast road, the level crossing being protected by a set of traffic lights as at Baldromma. Although this is the main coast road it appears to be little more than a country lane. Tunnel car 5, which still retains its original double windscreen, and trailer are heading towards Laxey on the level crossing. The fields of Ballabeg farm, which gave its name to the tram halt, lie behind the tram, and the farm buildings are visible above the cab near the clerestory. *(Vic Nutton, Courtesy Travel Lens Photographic, 1960s)*

This view is taken from near the updated traffic light system so as to avoid trespass on the railway. It is Easter Sunday and the island's 'Rush Hour on the Railways' event provides a high-intensity service on the Manx Electric Railway. Extra cars are in service to satisfy the enthusiasts, which explains the early season appearance of open motor 32 in command of trailer 43 on a northbound service. The motorman, on his exposed front platform, is dressed accordingly in a windproof uniform jacket, hat, safety glasses and leather gloves. *(5 April 2015)*

A low level shot captures the bulk of winter saloon 22, whose trailer is visible only by its footboard. This is the original car 22, whose bodywork was destroyed by fire at Derby Castle depot in 1990, and not the replacement built a couple of years later (see bottom right). To the right of the tram a field runs the short distance to the cliff top, but inland the main coast road runs roughly parallel to the tramway. In the background the tram shelter appears to have its windows boarded up. *(Vic Nutton, Courtesy Travel Lens Photographic, 1967)*

Winter saloon 20 and a northbound car set headed by a sister winter saloon have stopped for a crew change. Crew changes take place to ensure that platform staff return to their starting points at the end of their day even if their trams do not. A different perspective, which also avoids trespass on the line, is provided by the view from the trailer. *(31 May 2015)*

Heading south over the level crossing is original motor car 1 of 1893, with trailer. The motorman is keeping his eye firmly on the traffic as the van is well in front of the traffic lights. The van appears to be a Ford E83W 10cwt van, production of which ceased in 1957; it was popular with many commercial users at that time. At this crossing the local AC electricity supply wires pass above the DC wires of the MER. Guard wires, as installed for the telephone wires at Baldromma (see page 41), are not fitted here; presumably the circuit breakers on the system would protect against any accidental contact? *(Vic Nutton, Courtesy Travel Lens Photographic, 1964)*

Winter saloon 22 crosses the road protected by the traffic lights. Despite the much greater levels of traffic nowadays (and the hopes of the photographer) no ubiquitous white van arrived to provide a modern comparison to the van in the previous photograph. *(25 March 2016)*

Open motor 25 with trailer passes the crossover at Fairy Cottage; the crossover is normally only used when single line working is in operation. The sign on the waiting shelter on the right informs prospective passengers that, like almost all the tram stops, this is a request stop, thus requiring a clear signal to be given to the motorman. The main road, which is close by but above the tramway, is reached by a footpath to the left of the photographer. The car set has just passed a traction pole with a light that illuminates the footpath in the hours of darkness. *(Vic Nutton, Courtesy Travel Lens Photographic, 1964)*

Towards the end of the 2015 operating season winter saloon 19 and trailer 46 climb past Fairy Cottage. Trailers are often dispensed with at this time of year as passenger numbers do not usually require their added capacity. The tramway now rarely operates during darkness so the light above the footpath has been removed. The crossover was renewed a few years ago and was one of the first sections of MER track to be laid with Pandrol clips. The waiting shelter has been refurbished and the sign is now on the wall, rather than above the door. The new sign is digitally lettered on plastic rather than traditionally sign-written on board, but still looks fine and will probably last longer. Although Fairy Cottage is still a request stop it is no longer deemed necessary to emphasise the fact. *(11 October 2015)*

A few poles further down the hill from Fairy Cottage the tramway crosses Old Laxey Hill at Preston's Crossing. This is not the main coast road, which avoids Old Laxey by looping inland along the New Road. Looking down from near the junction at the top of Old Laxey Hill winter saloon 19 is crossing the road with a southbound service. In the 1960s many families did not own a car and the Vespa scooter on the road was probably a prized possession. It post-dates the tram by about 50 years. *(Vic Nutton, Courtesy Travel Lens Photographic, 1964)*

The view is similar today. Winter saloon 21 is heading north on the crossing; heading this way the motorman's sight lines are better. Increasing affluence shows that the motor scooter of old has been superseded by a more capacious Volkswagen, which is parked close to the crossing. The island's coastal footpath, *Raad ny Foillan* (Way of the Gull), also descends this hill, as seen by the waymark sign on the right. The traffic calming scheme in Old Laxey uses non-standard snail warning signs, below the 20mph roundel, whose meaning is very clear. Frustratingly the increased traffic on Old Laxey Hill can mean a long wait for car-free pictures. *(11 October 2015)*

Tunnel car 5 and one of the winter saloon trailers, 57 or 58, are climbing up from Laxey towards South Cape. Unusually car 5 has two headlights, which it carried between 1972 and 1981. Beyond the tram there are clear views into the Laxey Valley, with Glen Road and the Laxey River visible. Despite the bright sunshine in the Laxey Valley there is low cloud over the hills behind. *(Vic Nutton, Courtesy Travel Lens Photographic, 1974)*

The present-day view shows winter saloon 22 making the same climb. Tree growth has now all but obliterated the view of the valley from the wall above the tramway. Extra vegetation to the photographer's left has required him to take a lower viewpoint to produce the best possible match to the 1974 view, rather than a close up shot of a clump of ivy! The annual Manx Transport Heritage Festival is taking place so car 22 is not in public service but is engaged in motorman experience lessons and will return from Garwick. The cloud is lower today hiding more of the background. *(2 August 2015)*

Looking towards Douglas from the same elevated position open motor 26 and trailer have left South Cape and are traversing the level crossing as they continue their journey downhill towards Laxey. Unusually for MER stops South Cape is situated between two road crossings and is reached by a path from either direction. This is Miller's Crossing, but there is no name associated with the crossing of Old School Hill on the Douglas side of South Cape. *(Courtesy Travel Lens Photographic, 1960s)*

Taken from a few yards higher up the hill, but leaning over the same wall and overlooking the tramway, winter saloon 19 and trailer 40 are also about to coast down the long hill to Laxey. During 2013 a few of the MER cars carried commemorative vinyls on their dash panels to celebrate the tramways 120th anniversary. After removal of the vinyls, the car numbers were reinstated on the centre of the dash panels, whereas the standard practice is to align the numbers with the centreline of the car. Car 19 was one of the trams affected with the off-centre lettering. *(2 August 2015)*

The location for the Laxey Valley views seen on page 55 is in the background of this picture, roughly where the couple are standing. Are they watching the photographer or admiring the tram? The windscreen wiper will not be very effective where it is parked on the corner pillar of the body. *(Vic Nutton, Courtesy Travel Lens Photographic, 1964)*

The matching view of winter saloon 19 and trailer 41 shows the same tram at the same place doing the same job half a century later. It's interesting to note the subtle variations in the way the wire has been hung and, consequently, the positioning of the trolley wheel on it. The windscreen wiper has also now been fixed! The cattle guard also appears to have been replaced. The photographer is not under scrutiny on this occasion: perhaps people are more accustomed to tram enthusiasts toting cameras? *(12 April 2015)*

In the 1970s, original motor car 1 was often used as an engineers' car and, in order to provide some weather protection, somewhat rudimentary windscreens were provided at each end of the car. Hardly the most elegant fitment seen on the MER, but a pragmatic solution for the staff involved. Car 1 is paired with one of the earlier lightweight trailers, from 1893-4, distinguishable by the fact that only alternate uprights are full height, meaning that shutters cannot be fitted. Splendid on a nice warm day but offering scant weather protection in the rain. The car set is departing from South Cape with a southbound service. *(Courtesy Travel Lens Photographic, 1970s)*

Also on a southbound service is paddlebox motor 16, running with matching green-painted trailer 60. It is a bright sunny day during TT week with all available rolling stock running. The photographer has signalled his intention to board to the driver and the conductor peers round the side of the car to see who the intending passenger is. This view, although not an exact match for the one above, offers an unusual look at the paddlebox motor's footboard arrangement. *(7 June 2015)*

Original motor car 1 and lightweight trailer stand in the doorway of Laxey shed ready to pull forward onto the headshunt, while on the right hand road paddlebox motor 26 is attended to by a staff member who is probably checking the content of the sandbox beneath the driver's bench. This is the second Laxey shed, which replaced the original car shed destroyed by fire in 1930. At the time of the photograph the Manx Electric Railway was far busier, and several car sets would be put into service from Laxey at peak periods. *(Ted Gray, Courtesy Travel Lens Photographic, June 1962)*

Winter saloon 21 and trailer 46 are shunting out of Laxey shed ready to take up the first service of the day. After reversing in the headshunt they will run empty to Laxey Station and form the 09:10 service to Ramsey. During 2015, Ramsey shed was not used to stable a car set overnight and the 9:10 working enabled the first Ramsey to Douglas service to leave at the same time as it would have done if stabled at Ramsey. As a bonus, local passengers were provided with an earlier service to Ramsey. This is the third shed to stand on the site; the new steel portal-frame structure replaced the severely corroded 1930 building in 2009. *(24 September 2015)*

Inside the Laxey car shed motor car 2 stands in front of an open motor, a trailer and a tower wagon. Car 2 has a pair of hooks on the side of the underframe and these were often used to carry a ladder when engaged on engineering duties. Unusually the tow bar has been left in the Hughes coupler and an oil lamp is supported on the bracket on the dash. Against the far wall is one of the disused freight trailers, converted from one the batch of four motor cars, 10-13, delivered in 1895. *(Courtesy Travel Lens Photographic, 1950s)*

The present-day picture of the inside of the car shed shows two number 26s together. Open motor 26 is standing in almost the same position as the open motor in the previous photograph, while grey painted freight trailer 26 is behind. Sadly neither is serviceable at the moment. On the left, with 'wasp' stripes to aid its visibility is sister motor 27, which was previously used by the engineering department and carries windscreens for crew protection. Car 27 has no bogies, these having been lent to the diesel-electric works locomotive 34. On the further roads are a couple of other open motor cars. *(24 September 2015)*

The headshunt outside Laxey car shed has two car sets parked on it, car 1 and trailer are at the dead end, while open motor 29 and lightweight trailer are nearer the shed itself. Both motor cars have their poles turned ready for their next moves. In the absence of tell-tale shadows there are no clues as to the time of day, but it is probably mid-afternoon and the car sets are parked up awaiting the descent of the tourists from Snaefell. The trams will then shunt back to Laxey ready to return the crowds to Douglas in time for tea. *(Ted Gray, Courtesy Travel Lens Photographic, June 1962)*

An unusual shot of the tramway when there is no passenger service operating - note the rusty running surfaces of the railheads. The headshunt now holds MER truck 8, the permanent way flat 45, a tarpaulined Simplex diesel and a ballast hopper. During the winter, 2013-4, the station layout in Laxey Station was totally re-laid and the engineers parked their works vehicles here. Open wagon 8 has since been fully restored by volunteers from the Laxey and Lonan Heritage Trust and has acquired new body sides and ends. It appears on photographic charters and special occasions to demonstrate the historic appearance of MER freight trains. *(23 March 2014)*

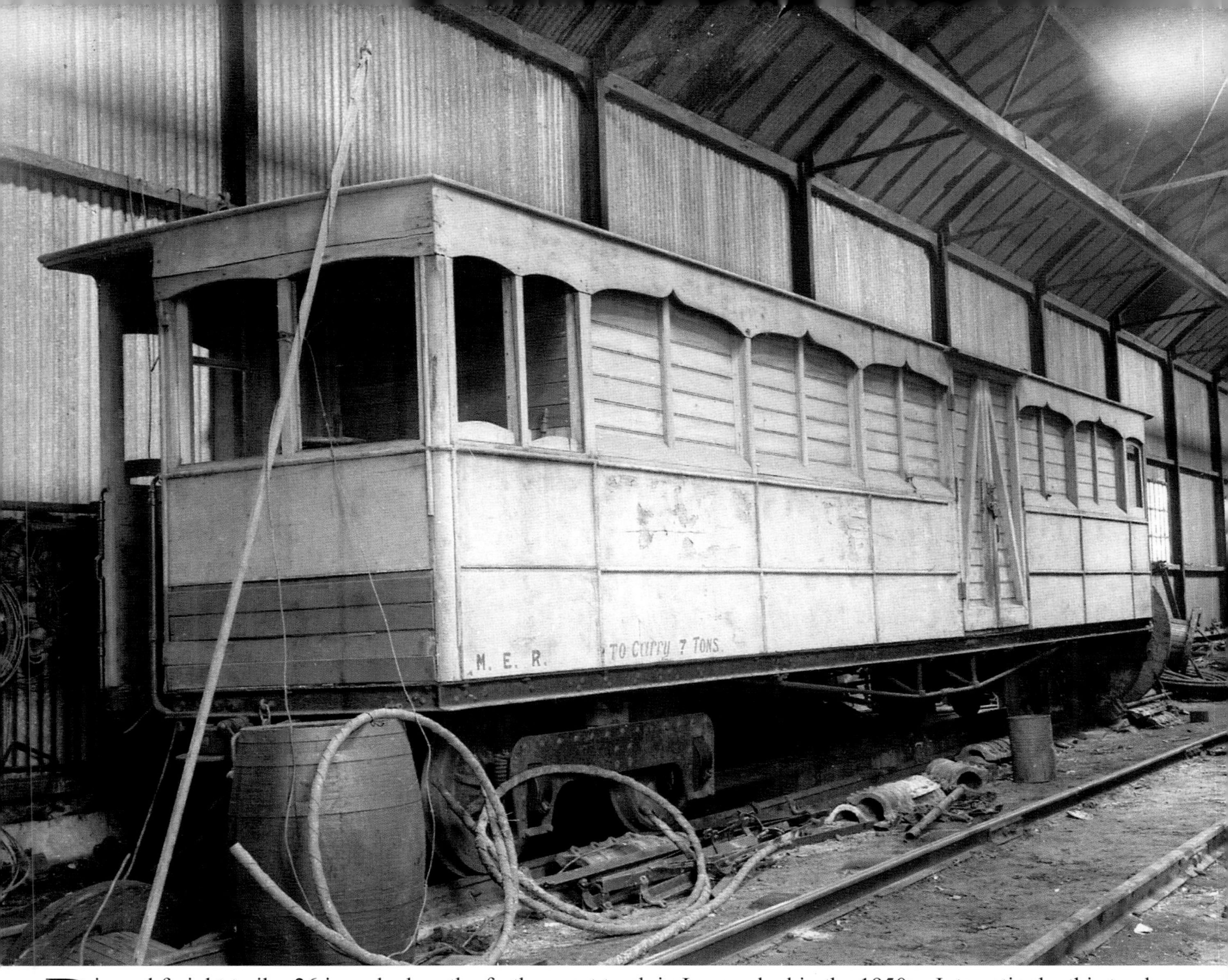

Disused freight trailer 26 is parked on the furthermost track in Laxey shed in the 1950s. Interestingly, this track was not accessible from the fan at the Douglas end of the shed, but could only be reached by passing through the shed and reversing in the yard at the Laxey end, near Rencell Hill. Given the lack of easy access this track tended to house infrequently required rolling stock. The tram looks neglected, but is in far better condition than its sister at Dhoon Quarry (see page 91). *(Courtesy Travel Lens Photographic, 1950s)*

Despite the appearance of neglect in the previous photograph freight trailer 26 is a remarkable survivor. Stored for many years in Ramsey shed the trailer was brought back to Laxey when the Ramsey shed was cleared at the end of the 2014 season (after which the Ramsey shed was expected to be demolished). After care and attention, trailer 26 is here parked at the back of Laxey shed. During the Manx Transport Heritage Festival in 2015 she even made a rare outdoors appearance in the Rencell Hill yard. *(24 September 2015)*

It is over forty years since ratchet car 15 has been used in service on the MER, but here it is seen with a lightweight trailer parked in the Laxey car shed headshunt. In the background another open motor awaits its next turn of duty in the open doorway. The shadows show that this is near mid-day so car 15 and its trailer are likely to be waiting for traffic demands at Laxey Station. *(Ted Gray, Courtesy Travel Lens Photographic, June 1962)*

Car 21 has just propelled trailer 46 out of Laxey car shed onto the headshunt. It is first thing in the morning and the car set is about to head into Laxey to form the first passenger service of the day. The set will end its duty at Derby Castle this evening. Duties are arranged so that trams do not normally spend more than one night away from the maintenance facilities at Derby Castle, but crew changes during the day return the platform staff to their starting points. *(24 September 2015)*

Winter saloon 19 and trailer have descended from South Cape and will shortly clatter over the pointwork leading to the depot and the adjacent crossover as they head towards Laxey. On the right, the headshunt is almost level so that unbraked vehicles cannot run back towards the depot. Access to the depot requires a double reversal from the northbound track and the headshunt, so there is no possibility of a tram running away from South Cape and wreaking havoc with the content of the car shed. The trackwork was renewed at the same time as the depot in 2009, and heavier section rail used in the shed itself. *(Ted Gray, Courtesy Travel Lens Photographic, August 1962)*

The Rush Hour on the Railways event suffered a mishap in 2014 when trailer 51 had a minor derailment on the new crossover at Dumbell's Row, temporarily blocking the lines just north of Laxey. Car 5 with trailer 47 was heading north and had to perform an unusual shunt, with passengers on board, at Laxey car shed. Car 5 reversed into the headshunt allowing its trailer to be rolled down so that it could be propelled into Laxey Station, which no longer has any crossovers. The service was terminated at Laxey and the car set returned to Douglas. Taken from trailer 47, car 5 is emerging from the headshunt to couple up. *(20 April 2014)*

On the south side of the car shed, a footpath crosses the line, joining the New Road at the top with Glen Road at the bottom of Laxey valley. Car 22 and trailer are approaching the crossing with a southbound service. An oil lamp hangs from the front dash. In the background the doors of Laxey car shed are open with a couple of waiting car sets outside; one staff member wearing the regulation dust jacket stands by the door and another is on the front platform of the tram standing in the doorway. Perhaps the car set will shortly shunt onto the main line? *(Ted Gray, Courtesy Travel Lens Photographic, June 1962)*

Looking from the same footpath crossing, tunnel car 7, which was substantially rebuilt in 2009-10, is climbing up from Laxey. Car 7 bears blue and white livery and is normally paired with similarly painted trailer 48. Today however it is in charge of non-matching red and white liveried 46. Car 7 is fitted with a high intensity halogen light below the dash which is an asset when the car is used in the hours of darkness. This provides a modern contrast with the oil lamp technology of the previous view. *(19 July 2015)*

After passing the car shed, the tramway crosses Rencell Hill on a bridge and passes the electrical substation before swinging round to cross Glen Roy on the viaduct to enter Laxey Station. The railings of the Rencell Hill road bridge are visible behind paddlebox motor 27 and its trailer, which have just passed the old mercury arc rectifier substation situated in a building out of sight on the right. Stacked on both sides of the line are stocks of rails. *(Dennis Gill, Courtesy Travel Lens Photographic, 1950s)*

The mercury arc rectifier was superseded by more modern power supplies for both the Manx Electric and Snaefell lines after the end of the 2013 season. Tunnel Car 6 and trailer 44 have just passed the new substation, which is out of sight behind the parked cars. The area is no longer used for bulk storage of permanent way materials. The photograph was taken from the access road which is sometimes used for delivery of items to the railway. The new power supply cables, which feed both the Snaefell and Manx Electric lines, are suspended from the traction poles on their way to Laxey Station. *(16 August 2015)*

Snaefell car 1 is foremost in this shot. Behind it on the left, paddlebox open motor 25 has turned its trolley and is waiting to use the crossover to position itself on the Douglas side of the trailer which can be glimpsed beyond Snaefell car 1. As the platform staff are not on board the tram they are probably waiting for the through car from Ramsey to pass before performing their next manoeuvre. A number of notices instruct motorists not to park their cars in the station. Increasing car use has made the problem worse, but surely motorists should not need to be told this? *(Vic Nutton, Courtesy Travel Lens Photographic, 1973)*

Following the removal of the station crossovers in 2014, shunting of trailers no longer takes place within the station limits, so trams no longer wait at this end of the station. Heading towards Ramsey, car 1 passes the spot where car 25 was parked in the previous view. The open-air licensed area of the Mines Tavern is now marked by a fence, rather than the row of white-painted barrels. In the left foreground the pointwork to the Laxey goods shed and the siding was removed during the remodelling. *(25 March 2016)*

Car 1 and lightweight trailer are waiting to depart for Douglas on what is obviously a windy day. Car 1 carries no fleetname, which may be a legacy of the tramway's economic difficulties in the 1950s. In the background there is a large wooden shelter on top of the concrete steps beside the Snaefell Mountain Railway terminus. The steps remain, along with many of the large trees, but the shelter was demolished many years ago. *(Tony Wilson, Courtesy Travel Lens Photographic, 1960s)*

Following the installation of the new track layout at Laxey in 2014 the stopping places for Ramsey and Douglas departures from the station were amended so that trams halted before they reached the enhanced pedestrian access path from the village, rather than where the crossing used to be. Car 1 is setting off for Douglas passing the spot where it was waiting in the previous photograph. In the background, Snaefell Mountain Railway car 3 is waiting to depart for the summit. Sadly this 120-year old tram ran away from the summit, with no one on board, five days after this photograph was taken, and was destroyed after derailing near The Bungalow. Fortunately there were no deaths or injuries. *(25 March 2016)*

Paddlebox motor 26 and trailer are waiting in the siding adjacent to Laxey goods shed for their next turn of duty, probably when the tourists descend from Snaefell on their way back to Douglas. Having run round its trailer in the station, the motor shunted it back into the siding where the car set is held until traffic demands built up. Meanwhile the crew relax on the front platform. In the siding behind, a flat wagon carries a supply of rails which are destined for the next relaying project. *(Vic Nutton, Courtesy Travel Lens Photographic, 1964)*

The siding was disconnected from the southbound line when Laxey Station's layout was revised over the winter of 2013-4. The former goods shed is currently used by volunteers from the Laxey and Lonan Heritage Trust, and often an item of rolling stock can be found under restoration inside. The yellow box van, converted to a tower wagon, is stranded, off the track, near the end of the siding. Inevitably car parking has taken over the space previously occupied by permanent way materials. *(25 October 2015)*

Beyond the Laxey goods shed the end of the line is in this yard. Permanent way materials are stacked on all sides and, in the middle, is works trailer 52. One of the early trailers, it became dedicated to engineering use in 1951. Its principal use was for transporting permanent way materials around the system. In 2008 trailer 52 was adapted to become the line's wire car and fitted with an elevating tower. It finds frequent use on overhead repair and maintenance tasks: for quick access it is kept in Laxey car shed so it can be dispatched in either direction when required. *(Courtesy Travel Lens Photographic, 1960s)*

The yard is still identifiable although the end of the then Corner Café has been demolished, the building made smaller and a varnished wooden conservatory added. Behind the blue car the former waiting shelter from the Lewaigue tram stop has been restored as an example of the traditional MER waiting shelters by Laxey and Lonan Heritage Trust volunteers. This was removed from Lewaigue in 1986 following damage by vandals and stored near the cattle dock siding outside Ramsey station for many years. The current structure at Lewaigue was erected in 1986. *(25 October 2015)*

Original 1893 motor car 2 and 'Royal Trailer' 59 are parked in Laxey goods siding at the Ramsey end of Laxey station. This was a favoured spot to leave a car set when demand for the Snaefell service was high, as the set could be called down for loading at short notice. The 'Royal Trailer' is so named because King Edward VII and Queen Alexandra were passengers from Douglas back to the royal yacht at Ramsey when they visited the island in 1902. The trailer is shorter than the remainder of the fleet and the short wheelbase gives a very different ride quality compared with the other trams. This interesting pairing of vehicles could well be a special working parked here while a party visits Snaefell. *(Courtesy Travel Lens Photographic, 1960s)*

The present-day view from the same point shows the goods shed *in situ* but with a rather less interesting collection of parked vehicles. The main line now lacks the necessary pointwork for railed vehicles to access the siding and the absence of overhead wires reinforces the sense of isolation. Parked trams are now accommodated in a new siding in the station. *(25 October 2015)*

As open motor 16 is obstructing the northbound main line, and the pole has been turned, it will take the crossover onto the southbound line as its next move. It is probably waiting for the next through tram from Ramsey; meanwhile the platform staff are taking a refreshment break. Possibly a trailer has been detached and, after car 16 has regained the southbound line, the trailer will make its way under gravity to rejoin the rear of motor car. Since 1998, car 16 has operated in the historic green livery of the nationalized era of the MER, but is seen here in the traditional lined red livery. Behind car 16, the name of the Station Hotel is prominently displayed. It was renamed as The Mines Tavern in 1972 as the building was originally the Mine Captain's house. *(Vic Nutton, Courtesy Travel Lens Photographic, 1964)*

When the station crossovers were removed in 2014, new traction poles and overhead were installed in Laxey station. As trams no longer reverse at this spot, finding a stationary tram in the same location is difficult. On the far track, arriving from Ramsey, car 1 and trailer 47 are cautiously making their way down towards the station buildings. This is the weekend of the Manx Heritage Transport Festival and car 1 provides special interest on the through service. The Mines Tavern has now had its new identity for over forty years. *(31 July 2015)*

A busy scene in Laxey Station. Tunnel car 7 is on the southbound line having run round trailer 45, which, under the action of gravity, is using the crossover to rejoin the motor. On the right the rear bogie of Snaefell car 2 is receiving attention prior to the tram's next excursion up the mountain. Note that car 2 still has the gate across the doorway rather than the door which was fitted later. A sister car is waiting on the far right. Interestingly this car has a permanent way wagon coupled in front; the handle standing at this end of the wagon is the screw hand brake. Any wagons are kept on the uphill side of the car on the mountain line so that there is no possibility of them running away downhill. *(Courtesy Travel Lens Photographic, 1960s)*

During the Manx Heritage Transport Festival Laxey is always busy. Just arrived from Douglas is car 2 with 'Royal Trailer' 59, while, on the left, winter saloon 19 waits with a southbound service. On the right, two Snaefell cars are waiting in the sidings. Car 1 was largely rebuilt in 2012 and appears in the blue and white livery applied when the Snaefell line opened in 1895. *(Sara Goodwins, 31 July 2014)*

Winter saloon 22 leaves Laxey with trailer, passing over the Glen Roy viaduct with a service for Douglas. It is evidently a splendid day and, in the background, Laxey Station has a large crowd of passengers waiting for the Snaefell line. The viaduct was one of the major structures built in 1898 when the tramway was extended to Ramsey: previously the Laxey terminus was near the car shed which was a short walk away from the village centre. *(Courtesy Travel Lens Photographic, 1970s)*

Heading in the opposite direction, winter saloon 22 is seen forty years later, with trailer 44 in tow. It is early in the season and the trees are still bare of leaves, giving a clear view of the station beyond the viaduct. Compared with the previous view the station area is apparently deserted. Although the bulk of the viaduct is formed of typical stone arch construction, the section over Church Hill, nearest to Laxey Station, was formed of steel girders with brick jack arches. The steel corroded so badly that this section was replaced with a new reinforced concrete deck in 2010. The parapet walls were reinstated and it is difficult to tell that the viaduct has changed. *(18 April 2010)*

Following the nationalization of the Manx Electric and Snaefell Mountain Railways in 1957, the new board of management chose a new livery. Open motor 33, together with matching trailer, is sporting the unlined green and white colour scheme. In the background Snaefell car 4 also displays its new colours, whilst another mountain car, just protruding from the left, shows the previous red livery. Only part of the fleet was repainted, and the decision to revert to the traditional colours was widely welcomed. The short-lived colour scheme can still be seen today as open motor 16 was repainted in the historic green livery in 1998, while its trailer 60 followed suit two years later. *(Vic Nutton, Courtesy Travel Lens photographic, c1960)*

Open motor car 33 is seen once again in Laxey Station but now resplendent in the traditional red and white livery of the Manx Electric Railway. In the background red-liveried post van 4 is parked in the new station siding, installed in 2014. As part of the Rush Hour on the Railways event, special railway postal covers are franked and carried on board the mail van during its outward journey from Douglas: those with an interest in philately may purchase the collectable items from the attendant post office staff. *(5 April 2015)*

Open motor 28, with super-lightweight trailer, draws to a stop in Laxey station as the motorman winds on the ratchet brake. Waiting to depart for Douglas on the other line is a car set including trailer 40. Much of the traffic to Laxey is bound for Snaefell with a change of tram here, but the MER is obviously keen for its passengers to 'extend your journey'. To car 28's right, and close to the boarding point, there is a prominent notice encouraging passengers to enjoy a trip to Royal Ramsey through the Garden of the Island. Of course extra journeys mean extra revenue so the MER has a vested interest in promoting the scenic route. *(Ted Gray, Courtesy Travel Lens Photographic, August 1962)*

Not an exact match due to the changed stopping arrangements in Laxey, but an interesting working. Waiting on the northbound line are open motor 33 paired with closed trailer 58. This is an evening special working which will terminate at the crossover at Lewaigue, a couple of miles short of Ramsey. Meanwhile the party of enthusiasts and the crew have adjourned to the station café for refreshments before rejoining the cars. Photo stops are planned along the line, with a return to Douglas scheduled to take place well after sunset. *(6 August 2014)*

Open motor number 16 and trailer are drawn up on the southbound line at Laxey. The trolley pole is turned for the next move, which will propel the trailer away from the photographer. The arrangement indicates that the car set has arrived from Douglas, and, having run the car round the trailer, the set is about to shunt into the siding by the goods shed to await the demands of the afternoon traffic. Note the line on the ground which shows that the car set has cleared the crossover. The manoeuvre also explains why the waiting passengers have not boarded – the tram is not going to take them where they want to go! Car 16 carries lining out, so is in the traditional red livery in this view rather than the unlined green and white which it now carries. *(George Hearse, Courtesy Travel Lens Photographic, 1960s)*

Unusually for the MER, the new permanent way laid in Laxey Station comprised grooved tramway rail instead of flat-bottomed rail. The new track was ready in 2014, but it took until mid-2015 for the refurbishment work at Laxey to be completed. The Laxey regeneration project interacted with the station works, incorporating improved access through the adjacent Rose Garden, the creation of a new village square in Whitehouse Close, new paths, and other works providing step-free access in central Laxey. With the new track in place winter saloon 19 and trailer 47 wait with a Douglas service. *(27 July 2014)*

DUMBELL'S ROW

Winter saloon 22 and trailer 47 head towards the level crossing outside the Isle of Man Road Services bus garage in Ramsey Road. In the early 1960s Laxey Valley Gardens transformed what had been the mine washing floors. The stone terraces for the former mine railway, the Manx Electric Railway and Ramsey Road are very evident. *(Vic Nutton, Courtesy Travel Lens Photographic, 1973)*

Tunnel car 7 and trailer 48, in matching blue and white livery, pass the same spot. Below the tramway a remarkable transformation has occurred. The Great Laxey Mine Railway has been reconstructed, complete with replica locomotives, and carriage and engine sheds built by volunteers from the Laxey and Lonan Heritage Trust. The railway passes below the road and the tramway in the island's only railway tunnel, which is of decidedly small bore. The flags prominently displayed are the Three Legs of Man and the Cornish flag of Saint Piran. The Captain of the Great Laxey Mine, Richard Rowe, was a Cornishman. *(26 September 2015)*

From a vantage point near the Snaefell Mountain Railway car shed, winter saloon 19 and trailer are about to cross Mines Road on the run into Laxey Station. Outside the former Isle of Man Road Services bus garage, which is off the left of the picture near the level crossing behind the tram, stands a substantial house. The access road to Glen Mooar looks new so perhaps the housing development in the valley has been completed recently? The traction pole nearest to the level crossing with Mines Road in front of the tram has white bands to discourage motorists from mistaking the tram track for the New Road. *(Vic Nutton, Courtesy Travel Lens Photographic, 1974)*

The present-day view shows sister tram 21, also with trailer, a few yards north of the previous photograph. Matching the location exactly would have lost the tram behind the advertising hoarding which invites tourists to visit the Lady Isabella water wheel standing about half a mile up the Laxey Valley from here. The substantial house has been demolished and the site is parking for Green's Garage, the former bus garage building. The additional street furniture makes the area seem a lot more cluttered. *(17 October 2015)*

The permanent way gang are busy on the tracks between the Mines Road and Ramsey Road level crossings. Note the absence of hard hats, safety boots and high-visibility jackets. Car 1, fitted with a rudimentary windscreen, is parked with an engineers' wagon. Behind the tram, the competition, in the form of an Isle of Man Road Services single deck bus, waits in Mines Road outside *Brown's Cafe*. Directly above the tram is the recently extended shed that houses the railcar for staff to access the air traffic control radio station on the top of Snaefell. *(Courtesy Travel Lens Photographic, 1970s)*

Winter saloon 20 and trailer 47 are passing the new crossover installed during the winter of 2013-4, when shunting was transferred here from Laxey Station. *(17 October 2015)*

Open motor 32, built in 1906, is approaching Minorca southbound on the descent from Bulgham to Laxey. The photographer appears to be standing on the rear platform of a preceding tram and another photographer stands at the end of the crenellations on the right. Evidently car 32 has been specially posed. The New Zealand national flag is on the left of the dash, but the other is folded and cannot be identified. The flags and the bunting on the tram sides show that this is a special working, but the details are not to hand. Behind the tram the course of the tramway as it climbs around the headland is clear and there are still fields to the left. *(Courtesy Travel Lens Photographic, 1960s)*

Replicating the position of the previous photograph was impractical, so this view is from the safety of the Minorca platform, to one side of the track. The crenellated abutments of the bridge over Minorca Hill identify the location, as car 2 coasts downhill on its way to Laxey. The vegetation has thickened and the route of the tramway as it curves round the headland is now obscured. The white house on the skyline in the photograph above still stands but is hidden by the tree to the right of the tram. Housing development has taken place on the left of the tramway as Laxey has expanded along Ramsey Road. *(25 March 2016)*

Winter saloon 19 and its trailer lean to the curve as they round the headland above Laxey. This isolated spot is sometimes called North Cape, analogous to the stop named South Cape on the opposite side of the valley. This is not to be confused with the northernmost tip of Norway which is a rather more famous and bleak North Cape! *(Vic Nutton, Courtesy Travel Lens Photographic, 1973)*

The modern photograph is not taken from quite the same location due to the presence of an inconveniently situated and very dense clump of gorse bushes. The motorman guides winter saloon 19 with trailer 40 once again round the corner above the northern headland guarding Laxey Harbour, and prepares to coast down the hill to Laxey Station. *(Sara Goodwins, 3 April 2011)*

Looking down towards Laxey a winter saloon and trailer have climbed past the Laxey Old Road stop and are nearing the headland. The footpath that serves Laxey Old Road is behind the hedge just above the tram, and climbs up to the Ramsey Road. The white house in the first picture at Minorca (see page 80) is just out of frame to the right at the top of the footpath. *(Vic Nutton, Courtesy Travel Lens Photographic, 1973)*

The same clump of gorse bushes which prevented an exact location match for the previous pair of photographs once again requires the photographer to take a somewhat different viewpoint. Winter saloon 19 and trailer 46 are climbing past the same spot. Abundant tree growth now obscures the line of the Laxey Old Road footpath, the main Ramsey Road and much else. Above the trees a group of modern houses with splendid views across Laxey Bay (on a clear day) can be seen to have spread across the fields. *(11 October 2015)*

Coasting down from Bulgham with its trailer past the Ballaragh stop is car 2, one of the original motor cars from 1893. Car 2 is looking a little neglected at this time. Interestingly a ladder is suspended along the car's underframe so maybe this is not a service car but is in the hands of the engineers' department. On the left can be seen the Ballaragh bus stop sign, which at this date was served by the yet-to-be-nationalized Isle of Man Road Services in competition with the tramway. *(Vic Nutton, Courtesy Travel Lens Photographic, 1973)*

At the same spot winter saloon 19 coasts downhill towards Laxey. The crossover was relocated a short distance downhill in 2008 when extensive track replacement was carried out on the northern section of the line. Meanwhile the bus stop pole now carries flags for both Bus Vannin and the Manx Electric Railway, both organizations being part of the island's integrated and nationalized transport system. Despite this Ballaragh is hardly a busy inter-modal transport interchange. Another sign of progress is the mobile phone mast on Bulgham Head behind the tram. *(25 October 2015)*

Just south of Ballaragh winter saloon 19 and trailer heading towards Laxey can be seen across a field from the main Douglas to Ramsey Road. The road and the tramway run parallel from Ballaragh, a short distance uphill from here, round the Bulgham headland; the turn into Dhoon Glen, the highest point on the line, is just visible above the gorse on the left. Behind the tram looms the hill of the Barony Estate. *(Vic Nutton, Courtesy Travel Lens Photographic, 1975)*

It is nearly the end of the tramway operating season for 2015, so winter saloon 20 has no trailer today and the gorse blossom has passed its prime. The neat painted wooden gates guarding a farmer's access across the tracks, have succumbed to galvanised steel replacements which, while undoubtedly sheep proof, are not quite so photogenic. In the background, the lighthouse at Maughold Head can be seen guarding the coastline. The few sparse trees on the Barony Hill have grown a little, but are still windswept. *(25 October 2015)*

The headland at Bulgham marks the highest point of the line between Douglas and Ramsey, and this location can be invigorating on a breezy day. Heading south, a winter saloon with trailer 42 is just about to enter the curve at the summit of the line. Round the bend the tram will be powered off and the brakes brought into action for the long descent to Laxey about three miles away. *(Vic Nutton, Courtesy Travel Lens Photographic, 1975)*

Also having climbed up the straight from Dhoon Glen to the summit are winter saloon 21 with trailer 41. There has been only one significant change at this location. Just out of sight behind the high ground on the right is a mobile telephone mast. The commanding view over Dhoon Glen and the coast road towards Laxey are an obvious location for a base station and a stark contrast to the Victorian technology of the MER. *(26 September 2015)*

MANX ELECTRIC RAILWAY
22

Travelling towards Ramsey (below) winter saloon 22 and its trailer have passed the summit of the line having completed the long climb up from Laxey. Just to the photographer's right and very overgrown is a low stone hut. It would appear to be some sort of store or other agricultural building. It seems unlikely to be a lookout point as it does not capitalize on the headland's eminence, but no one seems to know exactly what it was. *(Vic Nutton, Courtesy Travel Lens Photographic, 1975)*

Tunnel car 6 is paired with open trailer 40 in this autumn view as they round the summit curve and prepare to make the descent. Gorse is pretty, but invasive, and a lot was cleared in this area during the winter 2015-6. *(26 September 2015)*

Climbing up to Bulgham from the Ramsey side (above), is winter saloon 21 with trailer and one of the MER vans. The use of vans for goods traffic or mail was a common sight until the end of the 1975 season when the mail contract was relinquished in favour of road transport. Vans now make occasional appearances on the MER, but only for special events. *(Vic Nutton, Courtesy Travel Lens Photographic, 1970s)*

Although the view from Bulgham Head across Dhoon Glen (left) presents a countryside image, there has been a significant amount of development as can be seen by comparing the two photographs. Above the trailer the clump of trees now has a substantial bungalow as a neighbour, and the two small farms in Dhoon Glen below the tramway have both expanded. In the background a large new house has appeared beside the coast road which runs along the bottom of the hills; the tramway is on the seaward side of the road. Meanwhile winter saloon 22 and trailer 47 complete the picture. *(4 October 2015)*

Winter saloon 22 and trailer are approaching the sharp curve immediately before the Dhoon Glen halt. In the background Bulgham Head is at the end of the straight and the cars have just descended from the line's highest point. Owing to a slip in cataloguing, this photograph was accidentally mislabelled as 'Dreemskerry'. Matching it caused the photographer some confusion, as he at first wandered around a location five miles away as the tram trundles. *(George Hearse, Courtesy Travel Lens Photographic, 1960s)*

Tunnel car 6 slows for Dhoon Glen and its waiting passengers. Many of the present-day photographs in this book have shown how abundant the growth of trees and foliage has been but, in this instance, the greenery has been severely cut back and the main road is now visible up to the corner at Bulgham. Wild goat can often be seen among the trees on the left. They are not indigenous to the island, but are the offspring of escaped animals. The area around Bulgham and Dhoon is particularly favoured by these goats whose numbers have increased dramatically over the last few years. *(27 March 2016)*

Tunnel car 5 and trailer pause at Dhoon Glen with a southbound service. Dhoon Glen is an attraction in its own right, with a path to the cove, and the longest waterfall on the island to admire on the way down. There is a café here, which is obscured by the tram, and a waiting shelter. The tunnel cars had longitudinal seats when built, but car 5 had its original seats replaced by transverse throw-over seats in 1932. Studying the passengers near the front of the car they are sitting with their backs to the windows, giving the impression that longitudinal seats are fitted at this time: this is not the case. The additional suspension units fitted to the bogies confirm the correct era for the photograph. *(Ted Gray, Courtesy Travel Lens Photographic, June 1962)*

Sister tunnel car 7 and trailer 48 in matching blue and white livery pass Dhoon Glen. The original corrugated iron waiting shelter has been replaced by a newer wooden structure. Inside can be seen a table which provides under-cover accommodation for patrons of the adjoining café, which is the white building beyond. Car 7 was substantially rebuilt in 2009-10 and was also converted from longitudinal seating to transverse, similar to sister car 5 in 1932. This change was not universally popular. At the same time the additional suspension units on the bogies were removed. *(4 October 2015)*

A southbound train consisting of winter saloon 21, trailer and box van passes Dhoon Quarry. The siding contains one of the wooden MER open wagons. On the left is a stack of new rails and the unromantically nicknamed 'Creosote Cottage' stands in the middle distance. It was named such, as this was where the MER treated its wooden sleepers with the preservative, prior to installing them in the running lines. A couple of sidings, which served quarries on either side of the line, remain here. The inland quarry was served by a narrow gauge tramway, which passed under the coast road in a tunnel, and fed stone to the loading dock. *(Vic Nutton, Courtesy Travel Lens Photographic, 1964)*

Passing the same location is tunnel car 9 with trailer 47. Dhoon Quarry is still used to store permanent way materials, although the track and ballast are now placed on the right of the tracks where the quarry siding has been removed. The siding on the left holds two of the engineers' vehicles, a bogie flat wagon and a yellow-painted four-wheel wagon often used to transport the remains of trees which have been removed from the lineside. *(26 September 2015)*

Shunted into the loading dock are the decaying remains of one of the 10-13 batch of motor cars supplied in 1895. Their bodies were identical to those built at the same time for the Snaefell cars, which are still going strong after 120 years of hill climbing. Presumably the bodies were not deemed suitable for the MER as they were soon converted into freight motor cars and, for a time, used as cattle wagons. This one has been dumped for a long time and will eventually be scrapped on site. *(Courtesy Travel Lens Photographic, 1950s)*

The site of the loading bay and Creosote Cottage are discernible. Here a couple of side-tipping ballast wagons are parked where the decaying hulk of the freight motor was found many years previously. On the right there are stacks of new treated wooden sleepers awaiting installation on the line. In the past few years there has been a move to use concrete sleepers and continuous welded rail on the MER but these are by no means widespread – yet. *(26 September 2015)*

Winter saloon 22 and trailer are just passing Brown's Crossing with a service heading towards Ramsey. The sign by the road crossing points the way to the ancient monument of Cashtal yn Ard which is on a hilltop between the tramway and the coast. Car 22 has been fitted with an extra headlight, below and to the nearside of the standard fitment. The date supplied with the photograph may not be accurate as the trees behind the tram are leafless, which would imply that spring was very late in 1972. *(George Hearse, Courtesy Travel Lens Photographic, 31 May 1972)*

A short distance further north, open motor 33 and trailer 46 have just passed Brown's Crossing and are heading towards Ramsey. This photograph was taken during the Manx Heritage Transport Festival, when an intensive tram service is operated using the majority of the serviceable fleet. Open motor cars do not usually run on the Ramsey service, so this is not a common sight. *(3 August 2014)*

From the prominent brake handle in the bottom left of the photograph, plus the slight camera shake, this view of winter saloon 20 and trailer is clearly taken from the front platform of an open motor car. It is just north of Brown's Crossing, where the tramway runs parallel to the main Douglas to Ramsey road. Behind the winter saloon, North Barrule, the second highest peak on the island after Snaefell, looms in the distance. *(Courtesy Travel Lens Photographic, 1970s)*

Taken from the pavement rather than the tramway, the photographer has captured a pig! *Pig* is the diesel locomotive used by Manx Rail Projects. It has small wheels and a low maximum speed, but an extremely load hooter. It is late evening and the tram service has ceased for the day, so there is no porcine impediment to the trams or their passengers. The locomotive is returning to Dhoon Quarry sidings following a few weeks relaying track just south of Ballure viaduct. The TT fortnight is not far away, so it is essential to complete the track renewal and reopen the line fully to cope with the rush of passengers. *(21 May 2015)*

Winter saloon 22 climbs gently and is about to pass the Ballelin stop and farm crossing with a southbound service. Judging by the blossom on the bushes to the left, and the absence of leaves on the trees, this is an early season shot. A major storm struck the island in 2007 bringing down a number of the evergreen trees behind the tram, blocking both the road and the tramway and bringing the overhead down. *(Vic Nutton, Courtesy Travel Lens Photographic, 1975)*

Tunnel car 6 and trailer 40 are also heading south. The location is identifiable by the shape of the hills which, in the newer photograph, are only just visible above the tops of the trees. Although the trees have shown prodigious growth, the bushes to the left have been cleared and the sod hedge which separates the main A2 road from the tramway is well maintained. *(26 September 2015)*

Paddlebox open motor 25 and trailer have just passed Ballig with a southbound service. On the left the white wicket gate gives access from the main Douglas to Ramsey road across the MER to the field on the right. The tram is just leaving the end of a straight section of track, the check rails showing this to be a tight curve. A passenger on the trailer leans out, showing interest in the photographer. Due to the proximity of traction poles and other structures, the MER displays notices on all tramcars warning passengers that they risk injury by leaning out. *(Vic Nutton, Courtesy Travel Lens Photographic, 1967)*

The present-day photograph is taken from the footway beside the main road so as not to trespass on the railway. The gate has disappeared, but the gap in the embankment between the road and the tramway shows its location. Tunnel car 6 with trailer 40 is just entering the same check-railed curve. Note that the rail webs and feet are painted white on this curve. This is done at a number of locations on the MER and is intended to reflect solar radiation, so preventing the rails from overheating and minimizing buckling. *(13 September 2015)*

Winter saloon 20 and trailer are heading south and about to cross the minor road at Corkill's (sometime called Looney's) Crossing, which lies a short distance south of the Glen Mona stop. The absence of lineside vegetation gives a clear view to the north-east, with Ballagorry Farm prominent in the background. The farm is accessed by a private road which starts at the level crossing by the tram stop at The Garey a quarter of a mile to the north. *(Vic Nutton, Courtesy Travel Lens Photographic, 1975)*

Tunnel car 6 and trailer 40 provide the modern-day view, which shows that a driveway now joins the road just at the tram crossing. Below the tramway, to the right, lies a house quite justifiably named *Barony View* as the hills of the Barony Estate lie to the seaward side, across the valley. In the intervening years a screen of trees has grown up along the side of the tramway, hiding the most of the view, but Ballagorry Farm may still be distinguished through the gap left by *Barony View's* gateway. *(12 September 2015)*

Looking in the opposite direction, sister car 21 and trailer are heading towards Ramsey with a northbound service. The roof of a bungalow is visible above the tram and in the distance, roughly above the car parked on the left, Brown's Crossing lies on the edge of the hill, the tramway having swung to the right to maintain a more level course round the top of the valley. *(Vic Nutton, Courtesy Travel Lens Photographic, 1975)*

The present-day view is, once again, much restricted by tree growth, and the background, including the bungalow, is almost totally obscured by verdant foliage. Meanwhile the tramway crossing, like the majority of those along the line, has acquired yellow box markings and prominent 'Give Way' warning signs. The obliqueness of crossings such as this makes sight lines difficult for both road and rail users. The service is provided, once again, by tunnel car 6 and trailer 40. *(12 September 2015)*

Glen Mona is only four poles along the tramway from Corkill's Crossing. The simple wooden waiting shelter stands to the east of the line and someone has taken the trouble to clip the hedges neatly around the name board. At the Ramsey end of the shelter a Victorian post box is set in its own brick-built pillar. As the tramway conductors were sworn in as auxiliary postmen they collected the mail from the wayside boxes for onward transmission to the main sorting office in Douglas. With the suspension of the winter service, at the end of the 1975 season, this traffic was lost to railway when collection by road van became the normal practice. *(Courtesy Travel Lens Photographic 1960s)*

If it were not for the name on the shelter it would be almost impossible to think that this is the same location. The modern day view shows mature trees lining the route here with no view beyond the tramway at all. The post box has long gone and mail is collected from a box by the main road in the village: like many villages Glen Mona has now lost its post office. Meanwhile the old wooden shelter has been replaced by a rather more substantial version, and the name board for the stop is now mounted on the roof rather than on its own supports. The undergrowth is threatening to engulf the shelter, and is in stark contrast with the neatly-trimmed bushes in the previous picture. *(12 September 2015)*

Ballagorry marks the summit of the line between Glen Mona and the long run down through Ballaglass to Cornaa. Just north of the stop is the only overbridge on the whole line, which of course provides a good viewpoint. The bridge is an important piece of the MER infrastructure as it not only carries a local access road and footpath but also houses a substation, tucked under the eastern abutment. The bluebells and gorse are in bloom as winter saloon 22 and trailer coast down the hill with a Ramsey-bound service. *(Vic Nutton, Courtesy Travel Lens Photographic, 1975)*

In the present-day scene the growth of the trees is evident and the background is once again largely obscured. Winter saloon 19 and trailer 46 are heading north. The rails on the southbound line are rusty as single line working is in operation between the crossovers at Lewaigue and The Garey. Hidden by the overhanging branches at the top of the slope, Manx Rail Projects' diesel locomotive *Pig* blocks the other line as it is engaged in maintenance work involving improved drainage near the former Ballaglass Power Station. Behind the tram, the crossover at the top of the rise, visible in the other photograph, has been relocated about a quarter of a mile south near The Garey. *(13 September 2015)*

From the northern parapet of the Ballagorry bridge, the tail end of a northbound service is about to leave the cutting with a winter saloon in charge of trailer 46. Generally the earthworks on the Manx Electric Railway are relatively modest and consistent with the economics and capabilities of electric power on relatively steep gradients. This is one of the exceptions, and the deep cutting and the overbridge are an unusual pair of features. If the tramway had been laid to cross this road on the level, a steeper descent on the northern side would have been coupled with the need to build an embankment. *(Vic Nutton, Courtesy Travel Lens Photographic, 1975)*

Once again trailer 46 is heading north behind a winter saloon having passed under the Ballagorry overbridge, this time in the charge of car 19. Apart from the encroaching vegetation and some new traction poles there is little sign of any change during the passage of forty years. Some of the old poles can be seen lying beside the track. As they corrode they are often filled with concrete to strengthen them for a few more years use, and this can be observed following their ultimate removal. *(13 September 2015)*

WATSON'S CROSSING

Heading north from Ballagorry the tram track emerges from the other end of the deep cutting at Watson's Crossing. The halt takes its name from an MER employee who lived up the hill and crossed the line on his daily journey to the tramway's Ballaglass power station about half a mile further down the hill. Winter saloon 20 and trailer are leaving the cutting and are about to enter the straight leading down to Ballaglass. *(Vic Nutton, Courtesy Travel Lens Photographic, c1975)*

The present-day photograph is taken from slightly lower down the bank to avoid trespassing on a private garden. Tunnel car 6 and trailer 46 are heading towards Ramsey, and the motorman is giving the photographer a friendly wave. The traction pole in the previous picture has been replaced but the remains of its predecessor lie on the ballast between the lines. *(16 September 2015)*

When the Manx Electric Railway was extended from Laxey to Ramsey at the end of the nineteenth century, the technology for the transmission of electric power over long distances was non-existent. A power station was needed. As all power stations at the time were powered by steam it needed to be sited accordingly. Ballaglass was a suitable location, being near a small river to supply water for the boiler and conveniently near the mid-point of the extension. Coal was delivered from wagons on the embankment. Electricity generation ceased when the MER started to take its supply from the Manx Electricity Board in 1934. By then the use of high tension AC current enabled the easy transmission of power over long distances; it was then transformed and rectified locally to feed the tramway overhead. The disused power station is here seen from the railway embankment. *(Vic Nutton, Courtesy Travel Lens Photographic, 1975)*

During 2014 and 2015, steps were taken to improve the drainage of the MER in the vicinity of the old power station, with the intention of improving the stability of the embankment. One of the side effects was the removal of much of the undergrowth next to the track. Not quite enough to permit the present day view to be taken from the precisely the same location as the preceding view, as tall trees and undergrowth are only just out of frame on the left, but fairly close. The power station is now a private residence and the buildings are in a far better state of repair than in the 1970s. The extensive dwelling even has an indoor swimming pool. *(16 September 2015)*

Down the hill from the power station is Ballaglass Glen. In the heyday of the Island's tourist trade this was a busy stop, with a refreshment room in the glen itself. Winter saloon 19 and trailer are approaching Ballaglass with a southbound service, negotiating the reverse curve before the shelter is reached. Was the weather inclement on this day or was the photographer using the bracing to the hut's roof to make an interesting picture? *(Vic Nutton, Courtesy Travel Lens Photographic, 1975)*

The waiting shelter has been replaced but still provides a view of tunnel car 6, with unseen trailer 46, climbing up from Cornaa and about to swing round the reverse curves. The undergrowth on the inside of the curve by the footpath crossing hides the fact that the car is running wrong line due to drainage works (see page 99) *(16 September 2015)*

Having climbed up from the Cornaa valley, the tramway runs parallel to the A15 Maughold Road past Ballaskeig. This is open country and one of the more remote stretches of the MER, with the stop of that name designed to serve a couple of local farms. Car 22 and trailer are heading towards Douglas and are about to cross the farm access road to Ballaskeig Mooar which lies to coastward side of the line. The other farm, Ballaskeig Beg, lies inland of here. *(Vic Nutton, Courtesy Travel Lens Photographic, 1975)*

During the Isle of Man TT event the MER operates an intensive service and extra staff, many drawn from the management side of the organization, are drafted in to cope with the heavy traffic. Car 22, with a replacement body built after the fire damage sustained in 1990, is once again seen heading south. On the handles is the island's Director of Public Transport. *(9 June 2015)*

The view from Ballaskeig towards Cornaa includes the crossover which served here for many years. Although the view is looking towards Douglas, the large loop which the tramway performs round the end of the Barrule range of hills means that the photographer is looking almost north-west. The overgrown nature of the track is not best practice and is one of the less acceptable features of the tramway from this era. *(Courtesy Travel Lens Photographic, 1960s)*

The crossover at Ballaskeig was removed during the winter of 2013-4, meaning that nearest crossovers are at The Garey and Lewaigue, which can cause operational difficulties when single line working is used; it is the longest stretch without crossovers on the tramway. The changes in operating practices are interesting. In the old photograph there is no crossover wire, meaning that motormen needed to gain sufficient momentum before using the crossover and coasting across the points, with nifty work by the conductor with the trolley pole. Latterly a crossover wire was provided so that power could be taken during shunt manoeuvres. In the modern photograph the crossover track and points have gone, but the separate wire, which needed two depoling stints to use, remains in position, albeit unusable. *(12 September 2015)*

BALLAFAYLE CORTEEN

An unidentified winter saloon and trailer 41 are passing Ballafayle (Corteen) with a northbound service. The exit from the farm is not easy as poor sightlines for road traffic mean that stopping on the tramway before turning onto the road is necessary, which is not ideal. Despite the road being the A15, it is rarely busy, so any delay should be brief. In contrast with normal practice the trailer's emergency brake chain has been draped over the coupling rather than hanging in a loop below. *(Vic Nutton, Courtesy Travel Lens Photographic, 1975)*

Despite the passage of forty years the present day view is similar. The solid-looking stone gateposts were replaced over the winter of 2015-6, but the trees flanking the tramway are clearly the same as those featured in the old photograph. There seems to be an identity problem with this area. The latest design of MER stop flag, erected in 2015, bears the name 'Ballacannell', which was previously assigned to a stop two poles away. The new stone gateway is labelled 'Ballacallow', and this stop was previously known as 'Ballafayle (Corteen)'. Open motor 16 has attracted a number of photographers during the final trip of the day to Ramsey during the Rush Hour on the Railways event. *(25 March 2016)*

Winter saloon 19 and trailer are crossing the farm access with a southbound service. Next to the line is a small shelter: many farms provided their own which may account for the unusual design. This photograph was taken at the time when it was proposed that the Laxey to Ramsey section would be closed permanently, and this would have been the last season that trams could have been seen here. Fortunately sanity prevailed, the tram service was revived in 1977 and has continued ever since. The man on the left confirms that photographic interest in the MER is not a new phenomenon. *(George Hearse, Courtesy Travel Lens Photographic, 12 September 1975)*

Coincidentally the present-day photograph was taken exactly forty years after the previous picture. Single-line working is in operation, so tunnel car 7 and trailer 44 are running wrong line between Lewaigue and The Garey. For many years the farm buildings were not inhabited and had become a local eyesore. Despite appearances the house on the right is not new but one of the old buildings recently refurbished. The stone gate posts shown opposite have not yet been reinstated. *(12 September 2015)*

After Ballacannell the tramway lies below the A15 Maughold Road, but the highway gives good views of the tramway with the Irish Sea as a backdrop. A winter saloon and its trailer are heading south having passed the stop at Ballafayle Kerruish. On the extreme left of this picture it is just possible to distinguish the chimney pots of the Kerruish farmhouse over the hedgerow which forms the field boundary. Sir Charles Kerruish was instrumental in the resurrection of the northern section of the MER following the closure in 1975 and this is his farm. *(Vic Nutton, Courtesy Travel Lens Photographic, 1975)*

In the intervening years, hedges have grown up beside the tramway where only fence posts were visible previously, partially obscuring the view of the trams. Tunnel car 7 and trailer 48, in matching blue and white livery, are passing the same spot; on a clear day passengers are often treated to views of the Scottish coast from this stretch of the line. Behind the hedge on the left the farmhouse chimney pots are still just discernible. *(4 October 2015)*

Winter saloon 19 and trailer wait at Ballajora with a southbound service. The motorman has company at the front of the tram: the man with the flat cap is probably one of the MER maintenance team who has joined his colleague for part of the journey. Perhaps he is retrieving some tools from the floor of the tram? A couple of men attend to some bulky items of luggage, including a bicycle wheel, at the back of the trailer. Even today large items such a suitcases, prams or bicycles are carried here, with the shutters pulled down to prevent them sliding out. *(Vic Nutton, Courtesy of Travel Lens Photographic, 1964)*

Ballajora has one of the most spacious waiting shelters of the wayside halts on the MER, part of which can be seen in both photographs. At the far end, but out of sight on the left, Ballajora retains its Victorian post-box, the sole survivor of the lineside boxes between Laxey and Ramsey. The trees and hedges have grown but the chimney stacks on the house are clearly identifiable. The chalet-roofed house on the right post-dates the previous picture. *(25 March 2016)*

The broad sweep of Ramsey Bay leading to the just discernible northernmost tip of the Isle of Man at the Point of Ayre, lies behind tunnel car 5 and its trailer as they near the end of the uphill climb from Lewaigue, the longest straight on the MER. The photographer is standing on the edge of the Dreemskerry forestry plantation with the waiting hut out of sight almost directly below him. The wooden fence on the right protects waiting passengers from falling into the field beyond. *(Vic Nutton, Courtesy of Travel Lens Photographic, 1975)*

Fortunately some undergrowth was cleared in this area during winter 2015-6 and the photographer could reach the same spot for the modern photograph. The old wooden fence has rotted away and the modern replacement, installed in June 2015, is made of a less than rustic PVC equivalent. At this steep and oblique road crossing an extra white pole, formed from the top of a traction pole complete with finial, and white paint on the abutment wall end give visual guidance to road traffic. Open motor car 16, carrying green and white nationalization-era livery, slows for the crossing with the last tram of the day; it will be stabled at Laxey overnight, rather than continuing to Douglas. The car lights are prominent as it is nearly 6:00pm GMT and darkness is falling. *(25 March 2016)*

Having coasted down the long straight from Dreemskerry, winter saloon 20 with trailer passes the feeder box and is about to cross the road. On the left the Lewaigue signboard stands in front of the hedgerow giving the name of the stop. The original shelter here was replaced in 1986 but, after being stored at the former Ramsey cattle dock, has recently been restored at Laxey and may be seen near the goods shed. (see page 69). The shingled bungalow faces the road, which appears to be a very minor track at this time. *(Vic Nutton, Courtesy Travel Lens Photographic, 1974)*

The modern view shows a few changes. The bungalow is now accompanied by a garage with matching shingles which have just been re-treated. The sign has disappeared from the far side of the line and the vegetation on that side is being kept under better control. The feeder box has disappeared but there is still a feed to the overhead at the traction pole. Irritatingly, tram drivers heading south must power off immediately after crossing the road at the start of the climb to Dreemskerry. Heading north, winter saloon 21 sports a large Remembrance Day poppy. In 2015, the last day of the operating season was Remembrance Sunday although this picture was taken ten days earlier. *(29 October 2015)*

Heading south across the road to Port-e-Vullen is winter saloon 20 with trailer. On the left the old waiting shelter is just visible and, nearer the road, the post box is mounted in a brick pillar behind the fence. The Queen's Pier at Ramsey retains the buildings at the seaward end; although not visible in the modern view they have now disappeared. The photograph is taken from the track leading to the substation that supplies power for the northern end of the line. *(George Hearse, Courtesy Travel Lens Photographic, 1970s)*

The scene is readily identifiable by the low railings edging the track to the substation; they are the same in both pictures, although rather more dilapidated in the modern one. Winter saloon 21 and trailer 44 are crossing the road. Sadly the post box has not survived. Until the temporary closure of the Ramsey to Laxey section of the line in 1975, conductors were sworn in as auxiliary postmen and emptied the boxes along the line. With the end of the tram service, the Isle of Man Post Office switched to motor vans and many of the post boxes were removed. *(14 October 2015)*

The photographer has been lucky to catch two trams together... or perhaps not. The presence of another photographer in front of the bush in the middle distance, and the relatively large number of passengers for this stop, suggests that this may be a photostop of an enthusiasts' special. On the left an unidentified paddlebox open motor leads trailer 42 on a Ramsey-bound set, whilst winter saloon 21 heads towards Douglas on the southbound line. The crew member at the rear of the trailer seems very interested in the passing winter saloon. *(Courtesy of Travel Lens Photographic, 1960s)*

Winter saloon 21 heads south at the same spot, with trailer 47 in tow. In the background the vegetation now totally obscures the view. The waiting shelter was replaced in 2002. The local residents resisted the proposed metal bus-shelter style and a more tasteful, though unique to Bellevue, wooden design was redeployed from a previous use as a bus shelter at Port Jack. Unusually a smooth tarmac walkway has been laid between the 'platforms'. Some MER stops have these walkways, e.g., Minorca, and Port Jack, but they are not common. *(30 August 2015)*

A tunnel car crosses the Ballure viaduct on the last leg of its journey to Ramsey, winter trailer 58 making up the set. Riding on the rear step of the trailer in this fashion is risky, given the danger of striking one's head against a traction pole. The passenger is intent on looking through the decking of the viaduct, perhaps hoping for a view of the Ballure River around sixty feet below. *(Vic Nutton, Courtesy of Travel Lens Photographic, 1974)*

Winter saloon 20 and trailer 41 cross the recently refurbished Ballure viaduct and are about to cross the main road. The bridge looks spick and span following the previous winter's extensive works. The check rails outside the running rail are formed of re-used Fell rail from the Snaefell Mountain Railway, although at first sight they may appear to be traditional bull-head rail. Safety is more important nowadays – and not only for passengers. Note the barrier railings to protect those working on top of the supporting pier. *(16 September 2015)*

Work on the Ballure viaduct is not just a modern problem. Car 21 is crossing the main road at the traffic lights and approaching the viaduct, working wrong line from Ramsey. Obviously the southbound line is out of use so single-line working is in operation. *(Courtesy Travel Lens Photographic, 1960s)*

The 2014-5 repair work is almost complete. The cross girders of the viaduct have been replaced where necessary and all given new protective coatings. The waybeams which will support the rails are in place; these are not wood but, like many a model railway, are made of plastic. Rot prevention is assured where replacement would be difficult and expensive. The Manx Electric Railway closes for the winter and the work to repair the viaduct was scheduled for the closed season, taking most of the time from early November to late March. Final removal of the forest of scaffolding took a little longer. *(28 February 2015)*

A winter saloon with trailer 40 in tow heads towards Ramsey past the site of what is now the Queen's Valley stop. The houses have yet to be built on either side of the line, and Ballure Chapel dedicated to St Catherine, the roof of which is visible behind the tram, is still a place of worship. In the distance the houses of Walpole Road can just be seen where the tram track curves to the left to follow the street for a short while. Just in front of the tram, on the left, a gentleman appears to be taking a shortcut along the railway line. Nothing changes! *(George Hearse, Courtesy Travel Lens Photographic, 1970s)*

Forty years later and trailer 40 is still doing its job, hauled by winter saloon 19. The chapel has now been deconsecrated and is a private residence, with skylights cut into the roof. To the trailer's left the tidy patch of grass is part of the landscaping of the Queen's Valley estate which was developed in the early years of the twenty-first century. Responsive to local demand, the MER added a tram stop at the road crossing to serve the new residents; it is the only road crossing to lack yellow hatchments. *(30 August 2015)*

Having climbed the gentle slope of Walpole Road, winter saloon 20 and its trailer lean into the curve by the Walpole Drive stop and leave the houses behind. In Walpole Road, centre poles are not used and the overhead is supported by bracket arms from side poles. The original intention had been to pave the MER track in Walpole Road, and centre poles would have obstructed street traffic. *(Courtesy Travel Lens Photographic, 1970s)*

Tunnel car 7, painted in blue and white livery and lettered 'Douglas and Laxey Electric Tramway', with matching trailer 48, takes the corner. Street lighting has been installed and the overhead wires for the street's electricity supply have gone underground. The traction pole on the corner has been renewed and now lacks the splendid wrought iron embellishments of its predecessor. *(30 August 2015)*

Looking south from the Walpole Drive stop we see a winter saloon with trailer and van 16 heading towards Douglas. Hidden in the trees to the right of the tram is the Ballure Chapel dedicated to St Catherine (see page 116). Post van 16 returned to operating condition during 2015 following a long restoration process. It is now resplendent in olive green livery and appears in traffic during special events. *(Vic Nutton, Courtesy Travel Lens Photographic, 1967)*

Winter saloon 19 with trailer 40 head south. The area to the right has now been fenced off; the access to the former chapel is beyond the fence and the roof of the chapel may be seen through the trees. The trees in the field on the left of the track are now included in the back gardens of a suburban housing development. Further along, the Queen's Valley development can just be glimpsed on the right of the line. *(30 August 2015)*

Winter saloon 20 climbs the gentle gradient of Walpole Road having crossed Queen's Drive. The large green wooden building behind the tram is the erstwhile Beach Hotel, which, despite its name, was not quite as near the seashore as may be imagined. The Queen's Pier is about one hundred yards away to the right, so a short walk takes you to the sand. The hotel grounds extend down to Queen's Drive in the background. *(Courtesy Travel Lens Photographic, 1970s)*

The decline in the Isle of Man tourist trade has seen the demise of many of the island's hotels and the Beach Hotel is no exception. Suburban bungalows have now replaced the hotel, which are accessed by a series of entryways across the tram tracks. Interestingly, road crossings are marked with yellow hatchings, while access drives are not. Winter saloon 21 leads trailer 40 past the site of the hotel having crossed Queen's Drive. *(9 August 2015)*

Heading downhill towards Ramsey a tunnel car with winter trailer 58 also passes the Beach Hotel. Interestingly, the group on the rear platform of the trailer appears to be the same as that shown crossing Ballure viaduct on the same car (see page 114). Perhaps this is an enthusiasts' special working? It seems unlikely that the same car set would have been captured on film at the two locations by chance. *(Courtesy Travel Lens Photographic, 1970s)*

Winter saloon 21 and trailer 40 head down to Ramsey past the new bungalows and their gardens and will shortly cross the access to Clifford Drive and The Sycamores, which is where the entrance to the Beach Hotel used to be. The luxuriant growth of the trees obscures the splendid terrace of houses that still stands in Brookhill Road beyond the tram. *(9 August 2015)*

The penultimate stop on the Manx Electric Railway is Ballastowell, where a public footpath joining Brookhill Road to Waterloo Road crosses the line. Winter saloon 22 and its trailer have started from Ramsey, passing the car shed on their left – its end wall is visible above the trailer – and are crossing the footpath. Note the lamp bracket where a light illuminating the pedestrian crossing formerly stood. The approach to Ramsey is possibly the least picturesque part of the MER but the backs of the houses in Waterloo Road, although drab, are full of interest. *(Vic Nutton, Courtesy Travel Lens Photographic, 1975)*

Winter saloon 22 is again crossing the footpath and the empty lamp bracket still stands sentinel. In fact the biggest change in the intervening years is the tram itself – the original car body was totally destroyed in a fire at Derby Castle shed on the evening of 30 September 1990. The replica body was constructed by McArd Contractors of Port Erin and dates from 1992, as commemorated on a brass plaque carried inside the car. Compared with the previous view, the houses are more brightly painted and the chimney stacks nearest the line have all gone. The skyline has been cleared of much of the clutter of aerials and chimney pots, but satellite dishes have mushroomed to take their place. The tree which has flourished on the left of the picture, obscures both car 22's trailer and Ramsey car shed, which, although disused at the time of writing, still stands. *(30 August 2015)*

Tunnel car 6 and trailer are passing the Ramsey car shed on the left. A number of steel cables have been tensioned to add structural stability to the shed; from their uneven spacing they appear to have been added after the building was erected here. The shed was initially located on the south side of the Ballure viaduct adjacent to the temporary terminus of the line in 1898, and relocated here when the final extension to Ramsey opened in the following year. *(Vic Nutton, Courtesy Travel Lens Photographic, 1967)*

Nearly fifty years later it is pleasing to see that car 6 continues to serve the Manx Electric Railway, as the tram runs past the car shed on its way to the terminus. This photograph is taken from the Parsonage Road level crossing using a longer focal length lens, so that the pointwork leading to the car shed and the depot headshunt are visible in the foreground. Slightly worrying is the evidence of body sag on car 6, which has grown from being just discernible in the old photograph to rather more noticeable in the present-day view. *(Sara Goodwins, 4 April 2015)*

Car 5 and one of the two enclosed winter trailers, either 57 or 58, has drawn up before the crossing at Parsonage Road. This is relatively uncommon and usually means that there is a car set awaiting departure in Ramsey station. Passengers alight short of the terminus and need to cross the ballast, under the watchful eye of the conductor. On the left, the headshunt of the car shed has a piece of rail which is acting as a rudimentary buffer stop. Would this prevent a shunted vehicle from ending up in Parsonage Road? *(Vic Nutton, Courtesy Travel Lens Photographic, 1975)*

During the annual TT event, an intensive tram service operates to take crowds of spectators to and from Ramsey and the Snaefell line. The tracks in Ramsey Station can become full with car sets occupying all roads. Incoming services are then held on the far side of Parsonage Road, as has happened here with car 33 and closed winter trailer 58; the set is awaiting space in the station. On the busiest days a spare crew may be used to carry out shunting here so that the service crews can have a break. *(9 June 2015)*

Open motor 16 and trailer are about to enter Ramsey Station on the northbound line. Unusually, tunnel car 5 is standing in the cattle dock siding, where animals were loaded into the cattle trailers converted from former motor cars. This siding was latterly used during busy periods to hold spare car sets. The pointwork was removed during the 2003-4 winter track works at Ramsey and the siding buried in spoil. Presumably there is an enthusiasts' special event taking place as the camera and tripod on the bank indicates that other keen photographers are present. *(Courtesy Travel Lens Photographic, 1970s)*

The view above can no longer be repeated as the cattle dock loading bay no longer has accessible track. At the time of writing, a goods crane stands on the dock, although there are plans to remove this historic item to the transport museum at Jurby in the north of the island. Open motor 16 stands near the same place as in the old photograph, with the site of the cattle dock siding on the right. The intensive TT service is in operation, with a spare car set, comprising motor car 2 and trailer 43, awaiting traffic demand before backing down from the track outside the disused car shed. *(9 June 2015)*

Winter saloon 21 stands outside Ramsey car shed and the bogie is receiving some attention from the crew. Possibly the brakes need some minor adjustment? The shed doors are closed so it looks unlikely that the car has just emerged, and the shadows indicate that this is an afternoon view. Until the end of the 2014 operating season, a car set was usually stabled at Ramsey overnight to form the first southbound service of the day. Standard practice until then was to back the last arrival at Ramsey into the shed and shunt the trailer, if any, the following morning. *(Vic Nutton, courtesy travel Lens Photographic, 1975)*

There were plans to demolish the Ramsey car shed after the 2014 operating season had ended. Accordingly, all rolling stock stored in the shed was removed over the next few days and taken by low-loader lorry to Laxey. Winter saloon 22 was the last service car of the 2014 season and was stabled in Ramsey car shed overnight. On the day after the season closed, car 22 was used for shunting duties. Here it is preparing to shunt trailer 50, which had been incarcerated in Ramsey shed for many years, into the station for loading onto the JCK low-loader for a journey along the A2 road. *(3 November 2014)*

Once again a spare car set is seen parked on the track leading to Ramsey car shed. This time trailer 43 and a tunnel car are waiting: note that the pole has been swung for the shunt back to Ramsey station. *(Courtesy Travel Lens Photographic, 1960s)*

Another photograph taken during the clearance of Ramsey car shed at the end of the 2014 season (see page 125). Car 22 was used to shunt the long-stored cars down to the station for onward transportation. Freight trailer 26, not to be confused with motor car 26, is hauled out of the shed by an industrial diesel while car 22 awaits its next shunting turn. The batch of four cars, 10-13, had bodywork similar to the 1895-built Snaefell Mountain Railway cars. They did not remain in passenger service for long and were effectively withdrawn in 1902. Freight trailer 26 is the former motor car 10 and was converted in 1918. It is privately owned but at the time of writing it is stored in Laxey car shed (see page 61). *(3 November 2014)*

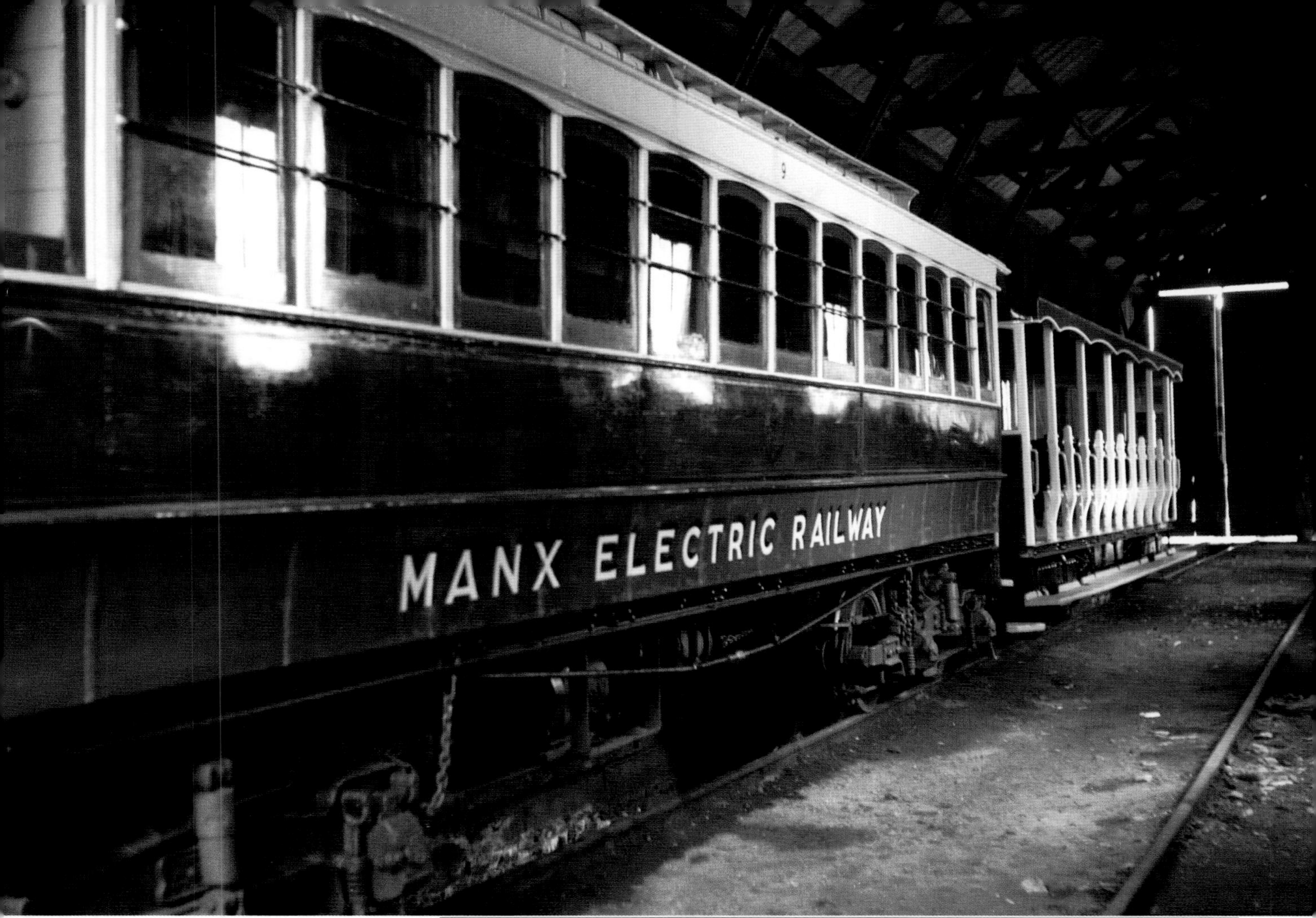

Tunnel car 9 and a lightweight trailer are dozing in the shadows of Ramsey shed. There appears to be strong sunlight from the right so this is probably taken shortly before the car set was backed out into Ramsey station for the first service of the day. Note that under car 9 there is an inspection pit. *(Ted Gray, Courtesy Travel Lens Photographic, August 1962)*

Ramsey car shed has been officially disused since November 2014, and this view shows the interior of the shed from the doorway, after the removal of the last item of rolling stock. The inspection pit visible in the previous photograph appears to have been filled in. At the time of writing there are plans to demolish the shed in conjunction with a scheme to provide a combined bus and tram interchange facility on the site of the current tram station. Shortly after the picture was taken the doors were officially closed for the last time, although the shed did play host to diesel-electric service locomotive 34 for a few months during 2015. *(5 November 2014)*

Tunnel car 5 waits departure time for Douglas. Surprisingly, the trailer is one of the two enclosed winter trailers (57 or 58) instead of the usual crossbench variety; a goods van completes the train. Unusually car 5 has two headlights. It ran in this condition between 1972 and 1981, when it reverted to the normal single headlight condition. When the photograph was taken the station building was only ten years old and retained the blockwork infill between some of columns. *(Vic Nutton, Courtesy Travel Lens Photographic, 1974)*

Motor car 2 and trailer 43 await the return of their crew. The TT event is in progress and an intensive service is operating. The TT course passes the inland end of Parsonage Road about one hundred metres away and the races are very audible from the station. The tram promises a leisurely ride back to Douglas with gently evolving vistas, in stark contrast to the TT's speed. *(11 June, 2015)*

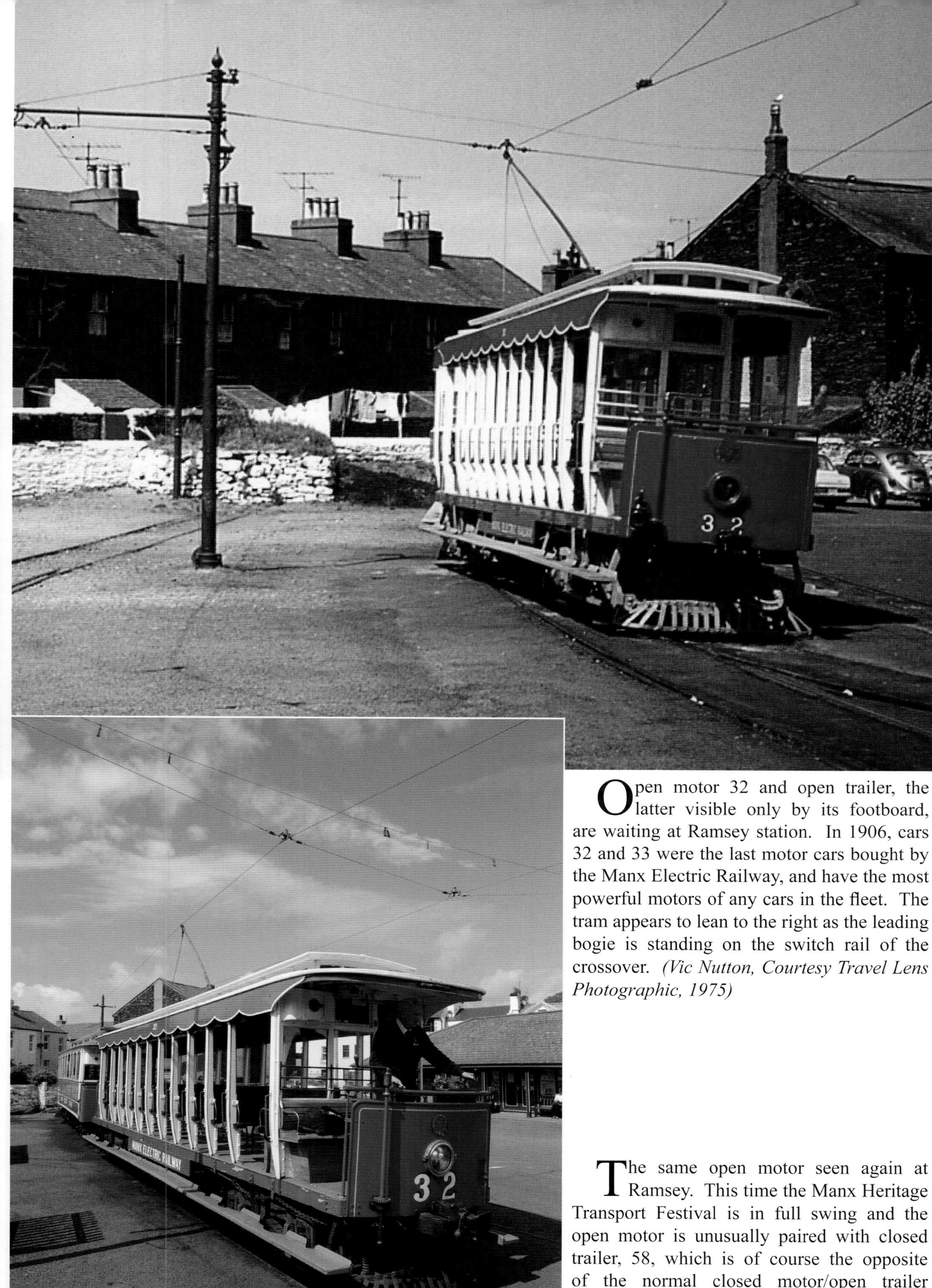

Open motor 32 and open trailer, the latter visible only by its footboard, are waiting at Ramsey station. In 1906, cars 32 and 33 were the last motor cars bought by the Manx Electric Railway, and have the most powerful motors of any cars in the fleet. The tram appears to lean to the right as the leading bogie is standing on the switch rail of the crossover. *(Vic Nutton, Courtesy Travel Lens Photographic, 1975)*

The same open motor seen again at Ramsey. This time the Manx Heritage Transport Festival is in full swing and the open motor is unusually paired with closed trailer, 58, which is of course the opposite of the normal closed motor/open trailer configuration. Unusually, the car set is about to perform a shunt move to take it from the normal departure position into the siding nearest the station building. *(3 August 2014)*

MANX ELECTRIC RAILWAY
16

Motor car 1 and closed 'Royal Trailer' 59, are parked in the siding nearest to the station building (left). An unusual pairing of motor and trailer and, as both cars are adorned with bunting, there is clearly something special going on today. This is the private charter by the Light Rail Transport League (predecessor of the Light Rail Transit Association, or LRTA) in 1956, and the trams have been shunted out of the way of the scheduled service operated by open motor 33. Not surprisingly the special has captured the interest of more than one photographer. *(Courtesy Travel Lens Photographic, 1956)*

Ramsey station shortly after construction of the current station offices and waiting room, which dates from 1964. The bulk of the Plaza cinema looms over the building, obscuring much of the background. In the station, a winter saloon and trailer await departure time with the next southbound service. Much of the outer perimeter of the walkway under the station building eaves is shielded with decorative blocks. Low cloud (or is it Manx mist?) obscures the Albert Tower on the hill behind the town, and the day is so drab that only the trams indicate that the photograph is not in black and white. *(Courtesy Travel Lens Photographic, 1960s)*

Open motor 16 and matching green and white liveried trailer 60 (left), have just started from the siding and are a few feet further forward from where cars 1 and 59 were parked in the previous view. The siding is rarely used and the trolley has dewired on the frog where the overhead wire of the crossover, which is normally used, joins the siding's overhead. The conductor has control of the situation and, from his perch on the rear dash, will soon have the trolley back on the wire and be belling the driver to restart. *(9 June 2015)*

Although the flag in the station area bears the name 'Ramsey Plaza' the eponymous cinema was demolished around 1990-1 and has long since been replaced by a car park. The station structure is still identifiable but the blockwork has been removed. Looking attractive, with hanging baskets and maroon paint picked out in white, the wooden supports now give a more open aspect. In the background, winter saloon 19 has just arrived from Douglas. On the hill the Albert Tower is clearly visible, and other building developments have taken place. Although the old goods shed is still standing at the time of writing (spring 2016), it may be demolished in the near future as part of the bus-tram interchange redevelopment proposals. *(11 October 2015)*

The normal practice for shunting at Ramsey is that the motor car uncouples, runs forward and reverses over the crossover to allow the trailer to roll down to the end of the line under gravity after an initial push by the conductor. The motor car returns over the crossover and couples up. The car set is then ready to depart for the south. Unusually, winter saloon 19 and trailer are on the siding nearest the station building while trailer 41 is in the far siding. To park here, car 19 will have had to draw its trailer forward and have set back. This is only usually done if an intensive service is in operation and there is a need to clear the incoming line. *(Courtesy Travel Lens Photographic, 1960s)*

Today is a very busy day indeed; it is TT week and extra trams are operating to cope with the spectators. Conveniently the TT course passes a short way inland of the tram station. On the far track, tunnel car 5 is paired with super-lightweight trailer 51, one of the original trailer cars from 1893, while open motor 16 and trailer 60 are parked on the line nearest the station building. Cars 16 and 60, painted in the historic green and white livery of the early days of nationalization of the late 1950s, usually operate together. *(9 June 2015)*

Trailer 62 is at the end of the line in Ramsey station with the shutters down, which is odd as the shadows indicate that the sun is shining strongly – perhaps there is a strong easterly wind. The trailer is headed by an open motor, just visible on the right of the picture. This photograph predates the construction of the current Ramsey station building in 1964. A rustic wooden kiosk similar to those found at Laxey or, previously, at Garwick Glen, stands beyond the car. In the siding beyond the tram a goods van waits its next call of duty. *(Courtesy Travel Lens Photographic, 1950s)*

In the same location 'Royal Trailer' 59 is parked at the end of the line, also in brilliant sunshine. This photograph shows the short wheelbase of the car in excellent detail, and goes some way to explaining the trailer's very pronounced waddle in motion. One of the lesser-used trailers, number 59 is in immaculate condition. *(19 September 2013)*

Winter saloon 22 is shunting trailer 47, which seems to be shyly hiding its real identity. There is no trailer 4 and motor car 4 was destroyed in the Laxey car shed fire of 1930. The Ramsey Plaza cinema building, which obscured the sight lines at Parsonage Road, is close to the track behind car 22. The visibility problem at this crossing is underlined by the proliferation of 'Danger Beware of the Cars' notices on the pole between the two vehicles. *(Courtesy Travel Lens Photographic, 1960s)*

The 'Rush Hour on the Railways' event features special operations on the Isle of Man Railways over the Easter weekend each year. One special event saw a simulation of the historic formation of motor car with trailer and post van. Shunting at the terminus requires reversal of the formation and takes an extra couple of shunts to place the vehicles in the correct order. Here, winter saloon 19 has shunted trailer 40, and the second stage is under way to bring the post van, goods stock 4, to the rear. The sides of the van are lettered 'I.O.M.E.T & E.P Co Ltd': which stands for Isle of Man Electric Tramway and Electric Power Company Limited (see page 136), the predecessor of the Manx Electric Railway and responsible for the construction of the original tramway in the late Victorian era. *(5 April 2015)*

Standing in the siding nearest the station building are paddlebox open motor 25 and trailer 55. As in the top picture on page 132, these cars have been shunted here rather than departing from the usual position. Sadly neither car 25 nor trailer 55 has been seen in service in recent years. *(Ted Gray, Courtesy Travel Lens Photographic, August 1962)*

Also standing in the siding are open motor 33 with trailer 46. A good load on board and one lucky passenger has the honour of sharing the front bench seat with the motorman for an unrestricted view of the passing scenery. With one hand on the air brake valve and the other on the controller the motorman is poised to start the journey south. Just visible at the normal departure point are tunnel car 5 and trailer 44. *(3 August 2014)*

The Manx Electric Railway handled significant freight traffic and owned a fleet of vans and open wagons as well as goods sheds at Douglas, Laxey and Ramsey. Much of this traffic was lost with the temporary closure of the northern section of line after the 1975 season. Standing in Ramsey station is a pair of vans. No 12, supplied by Milnes in 1898-9, has a 6 ton capacity body; it lost its roof in a storm at Ballafayle in 1967 and was rebuilt with a peaked roof. Van 12 later served as a tower wagon for many years and, at the time of writing, is awaiting restoration in Laxey goods yard (see pages 68-9). No 16 is a large mail van constructed by the MER itself in 1908. No 16 was restored in 2015 and may still appear in Ramsey on special event days. *(Vic Nutton, Courtesy Travel Lens Photographic, 1975)*

The Manx Heritage Transport Festival usually sees special demonstration freight workings on the MER. Parked in the siding at Ramsey are open wagon 10, built by Milnes in 1897-8 when the Ramsey extension was under construction, and post van 4, also built by Milnes but dating from 1895. Taken with a wide-angle lens which explains the odd perspective, the van's end platforms allow easy access from either side of the track. Behind the freight stock are open motor 32 and tunnel car 5. *(3 August 2014)*

Parked at Ramsey is a pair of drop-sided open wagons. The number 1 can be just be made out on the middle of the wagon side, this vehicle being supplied by Milnes in 1894 when the line was extended from Groudle to Laxey. The wagon has since been used in various roles by the engineers and is currently in store. The palm trees in the background were removed when the current Ramsey station building was erected in 1964. *(Courtesy Travel Lens Photographic, 1950s)*

Exchange of engineers' stock between the Isle of Man Steam Railway and the MER occurs when major projects are planned. This bogie ballast wagon was brought to Ramsey at the start of the 2014-5 winter closure, when repairs to the Ballure viaduct isolated Ramsey. The wagon is based on the underframe of an Isle of Man Railways 'pairs' coach, F70. 'Pairs' coaches consisted of two old four-wheel coach bodies mounted on a new bogie underframe. The road low-loader was used later that day to transfer rolling stock that had been stored in Ramsey shed to Laxey, including trailer 50 (see page 125). *(3 November 2014)*

Winter saloon 19 and trailer leave Ramsey for the south. In the background three goods vans are parked at the end of the lines in the station itself, together with an open trailer. On the left, but out of sight, Ramsey goods shed was still in use and may play host to more wagons. The Plaza cinema stands close to the MER lines on the corner of Parsonage Road. The photographer is standing on the old cattle dock with the points to the siding in the foreground. *(Vic Nutton, Courtesy Travel Lens Photographic, 1973)*

Tunnel car 7 and trailer 48 depart Ramsey for Douglas. The site of the Plaza cinema is currently a car park and the sight lines between the MER and Parsonage Road are much better, even though Ramsey has lost an amenity. Ramsey goods shed is still in place at the time of writing: until recently it had been used as a youth amenity facility, but at the time of writing it is disused. The proposed redevelopment of Ramsey station as a transport interchange may lead to major changes in the view from here in the near future. *(14 May 2012)*

The young motorman of car 33 certainly seems to be enjoying his work on this sunny day – and why not! This is during TT practice week so passengers are likely to be plentiful. Car 33 has probably arrived with a trailer and, having shunted out of its way, is now easing downhill to couple up for the return trip to Douglas. The current normal practice is for the conductor to wait with the trailer to couple it up. Possibly another staff member was on hand to assist as the conductor appears to be on the back platform. *(George Hearse, Courtesy Travel Lens Photographic, 31 May 1972)*

The annual Manx Heritage Transport Festival sees special intensive services on the MER and the less regularly used trams are out as well. Motorman John Cliffe, who retired at the end of the 2015 season, puts open motor 33 through the shunting manoeuvre, having allowed its trailer to roll down to the end of the line. The overhead is now supported by a traction pole instead of the wall of the cinema; note that the traction poles and building woodwork in Ramsey station are painted maroon, rather than the MER's ubiquitous green. The mirror on the blind corner of Parsonage Road improves the visibility between trams and road traffic and replaces the warning notices. Eagle-eyed readers will see the back of car 33 and the photographer in it. *(29 July 2014)*

ACKNOWLEDGEMENTS

The historic photographs have been mainly drawn from the collections held by Travel Lens Photographic. The assistance and collaboration of Tony Wilson is gratefully acknowledged: without his help the production of this book would have been impossible.

For her understanding during the collection and preparation of the material, editorial guidance, typesetting and bringing this book to its final printed form the assistance of my wife, Sara Goodwins, has been invaluable.

SELECTED BIBLIOGRAPHY

Basnett, Stan, *Trams of The Isle of Man 1946-Present Day*, Lily Publications, undated c. 2008
Edwards, Barry, *The Railways and Tramways of the Isle of Man*, Oxford Publishing Co., 1993
Edwards, Barry, *The Manx Electric Railway*, B&C Publications, 1998
Edwards, Barry, *Trains and Trams of the Isle of Man*, Lily Publications, 2010
Goodwyn, Mike, *All about The Manx Electric Railway*, Manx Electric Railway Society, 1989
Goodwyn, Mike, *Manx Electric*, Platform 5 Publishing, 1993
Gray, Edward, *Manx Railways and Tramways*, Sutton Publishing, 1998
Gray, Ted, *Railways and Tramways of the Isle of Man; a Past and Present Companion*, Past and Present Publishing 2008
Heavyside, Tom, *Douglas – Laxey – Ramsey*, Middleton Press, 2010
Hendry, Robert P., *Manx Electric Railway Saga*, Adam Gordon, 2010
Hendry, R Preston and Hendry, R Powell, *Manx Electric Railway Album*, Hillside Publishing Co., 1978
Hobbs, George, *Stops Along the Manx Electric Railway*, Loaghtan Books, 2014
Jones, Norman, *Isle of Man Tramways*, Foxline Publishing c 1993
Pearson, F.K., *Isle of Man Tramways*, David and Charles, 1970
Pearson, Keith, *One Hundred Years of The Manx Electric Railway*, Leading Edge Press and Publishing, 1992
Pulling, Chris, *Journey on the Manx Electric Railway*, Train Crazy Publishing, 2015
Scarffe, Andrew, *The Railways and Tramways of Laxey*, Mannin Media, undated c.2014

Journals and periodicals

Manx Transport Review, Manx Electric Railway Society, various issues
Trams Magazine, Train Crazy Publication, various issues

This builder's plate is on the Ramsey end inland side of the bridge abutment walling of Ballure viaduct. It credits both the designer of the bridge and the builders, who are also credited as building roofs. The viaduct spans Ballure Glen and was essential for the tramway to reach Ramsey about three quarters of a mile away. For about a year, and until the viaduct opened in 1899, the tramway had a temporary terminus on the south side of the glen. *(Vic Nutton, Courtesy of Travel Lens Photographic, 1971)*

Over the winter 2014-5 the Ballure viaduct underwent major maintenance works costing more than a million pounds. Replacement of wasted steel sections and rivets restored the bridge's strength, and the modern coating should protect the bridge against corrosion for at least thirty years. As part of these works the plaque was also refurbished. *(9 August 2015)*

After the refurbishment, the Laxey Blacksmith provided a new plaque in a similar style to the original. It is fixed to the seaward side of the viaduct at the Ramsey end, on the opposite side of the tracks from the original plaque. *(9 August 2015)*